tapas

pas

Louise Pickford

*photography by* Sandra Lane

hamlyn

First published in the U.K. in 1997 by Hamlyn
an imprint of Octopus Publishing Group Limited
2–4 Heron Quays
London E14 4JP

Distributed in the United States and Canada by
Sterling Publishing Co., Inc.
387 Park Avenue South
New York, NY 10016-8810

Tapas
Louise Pickford

ISBN 0 600 60097 1

Main text set in 10 on 14pt Linotype Sabon

Produced by Toppan
Printed in China

**Publishing Director:** Laura Bamford

**Editor:** Sasha Judelson
**Assistant Editor:** Katey Day
**Commissioning Editor:** Nicola Hill
**Americanization by:** Barbara Horn

**Art Director:** Keith Martin
**Senior Designer:** Louise Leffler

**Photographer:** Sandra Lane
**Home Economist:** Louise Pickford
**Stylist:** Mary Nordan
**Indexer:** Hilary Bird

**Production Controller:** Dawn Mitchell

## Notes

All recipes serve 4 unless otherwise stated

Eggs should be medium unless otherwise stated.

Milk should be whole unless otherwise stated.

Fresh herbs should be used unless otherwise stated. If unavailable use
dried herbs as an alternative but halve the quantities stated.

Ovens should be preheated to the specified temperature. If using a
fan-assisted oven, follow the manufacturer's instructions for adjusting
the time and temperature.

# contents

# introduction

At the heart of Spanish traditions is a ritual carried out daily with typical Mediterranean passion: the eating of tapas—a small snack washed down with a glass of chilled sherry or wine—takes places in bars all over Spain at both lunchtime and then again in the early evening.

The word "tapa," from which tapas derives, translates literally as "cover;" as the story goes, bar owners would serve their customers a drink with a slice of bread covering the top of the glass. This rather bizarre custom was most probably done for a very good reason: to prevent insects from enjoying the drink between sips! The bread was then eaten. Soon it became usual to top the bread with a slice of ham or cheese, and thus the custom of tapas was born.

For some people, tapas may evoke memories of vacations abroad. After a day relaxing in the sun, a thirst-quenching drink and a little nibble seem a perfect way to enjoy those last few hours of sunlight. Small tables spill out of the bars onto sidewalks and many a tourist and local alike sit and chatter cheerfully with a chilled drink in one hand and a plate of roasted nuts or chile-spiked olives in the other. Whenever I travel abroad I am instantly drawn to the street foods and snacks that are far more commonplace than at home. Many of these dishes are finger foods, making them practical to eat while meandering through the narrow streets. I find it much more interesting to nibble on a number of small morsels, with a range of exciting flavors and textures.

Tapas can, of course, also be enjoyed when entertaining at home. Whether you are hosting a cocktail party, a formal dinner, or a casual gathering of close friends, handing around a tray of finger foods will always be appreciated. As well as receiving praise from your guests, there are practical benefits in preparing tapas yourself. A few nibbles with drinks can often mean serving two rather than three courses at dinner; so the extra time spent on preparing the nibbles may well save you time later.

*Tapas* is divided into six practical chapters and offers a much broader collection of dishes than just Spanish-style tapas. Appetizers, nibbles, and snacks from all over the world have been brought together to produce a comprehensive recipe book with tapas for every occasion.

Each chapter is self-explanatory, offering the reader instant access to the type of recipe required. **One Bite**, the first chapter, contains dishes of small nibbles that can literally eaten in one mouthful. Recipes include Salted Almonds, Spicy Glazed Cashews, and Root Vegetable Chips. These really are the perfect partners to a glass of chilled wine or sherry, and should be arranged in small dishes or on napkins, to sit neatly on a tray or platter as the drinks are handed around. Toothpicks are useful to spike oily foods such as Marinated Olives, but make sure you have a saucer or empty dish to hand for the olive pits.

**Two Bites** provides a wide range of really exciting recipes with just that bit more to

them. Polenta Triangle Sandwiches and Cheese Stuffed Phyllo Fingers are ideal if you are hosting a cocktail party, when it is often a good idea to offer slightly more substantial dishes to eat. Tasty food and good wine are, after all, convivial to happy banter and a successful party! Interesting new recipe ideas can be found here, including Chile-Fried Panisse and Smoked Mussel Fritters.

The third chapter, **Bigger Bites**, offers dishes that are ideal as a light lunch or supper dish, and can also be served as an appetizer. Alternatively, lay out a selection of five or six dishes "meze-style" so everyone can help themselves. There are some old favorites to be found here, like the Piedmontese Peppers and Spanish Tortilla, intermingled with a few more unusual recipes, such as the Anchovy-stuffed Zucchini Flowers and Rolled Skewered Sole Fillets with Tomatoes and Mozzarella.

**Little Dishes** epitomizes Spain and the tapas tradition more than any other chapter, with its collection of dishes served in small bowls, plates, and saucers (or, in some cases, shells) in a typical Spanish manner. Unlike most of the other chapters, however, you will need a fork to eat the food. These recipes are versatile and lend themselves perfectly to a casual dinner, when you could serve perhaps six different dishes. As the emphasis is Spanish, you will find several classic tapas dishes, including Potato Bravas, Kidneys Cooked with Sherry, and Fava Beans with Serrano Ham. If you are feeling more adventurous, try the Pacific Rim Mussels or the Marinated Herring with Horseradish Cream.

Most of the dishes in **Breads and Pastries** are substantial enough to be served as a light meal, appetizer, or snack. There are several kinds of crostini or bruschetta recipes, including the unusual Shrimp and Arugula Piadina. A piadina is an Italian wheat tortilla, which was, in fact, the precursor to the pizza base, and it provides a delicious base for the shrimp topping. Several of the dishes make ideal picnic foods, particularly the Pan Bagnat Slices and the Picnic Chicken Loaf. They always look fabulous in the bright sunshine; just before you set off, wrap them in waxed paper, .

The final chapter, **Sauces, Oils, and Dips,** includes accompaniments to, or integral parts of, recipes found in other parts of the book as well as recipes in their own right. The oils can all be served with fresh bread to dip, which I think always makes a lovely appetizer and helps your guests relax around the dinner table. The Bagna Cauda (a classic Italian anchovy sauce) is traditionally served hot in its own dish at the table, but without that traditional serving dish I simply transfer it to a separate bowl and serve it warm with a selection of baby vegetables.

Despite this book's obvious links with a long-serving and wonderful tradition, I have tried to give it a modern feel, emphasized by a collection of international recipes and by the light and colorful photography as well as a simple, modern design. All of these factors come together to make a book that I hope will inspire cooks and satisfy the eaters!

Opposite from top left clockwise: Mini Chicken Kiev (see page 56); Roasted Vine Tomatoes with Goat Cheese (see page 90); Garbanzo bean and Chard Tortilla (see page 60); and Broiled Corn with Flavored Butters (see page 40)

# glossary of ingredients

**Bulgur wheat**
Bulgur is cracked wheat that has been par-boiled, hulled, and dried. This process enables the grain to absorb liquid more readily, reducing the cooking time. It is used extensively in North African, Greek, Turkish, and Middle Eastern cooking.

**Chard**
A member of the beet family, chard is a green leaf vegetable with a thick white central stalk, which should be discarded before cooking. (The stalks of red chard can be eaten.) Chard can be served as a vegetable on its own and is particularly nice when steamed and tossed with extra-virgin olive oil, salt, pepper, and lemon juice.

**Chorizo**
A Spanish pork sausage, chorizo is made with paprika, which gives it a distinctive red color. Chorizo can be mild or highly spiced, and is usually cured and can be eaten raw.

**Coconut cream**
More authentic than canned coconut milk, coconut cream is available in small cartons from some supermarkets or oriental food stores. Use creamed coconut dissolved in boiling water as a substitute.

**Dried fava beans**
Dried fava beans are available in supermarkets, health food stores., and specialist food stores. Dried lima beans can be substituted.

**Dried shiitake mushrooms**
These dried mushrooms may be available in supermarkets, and the larger variety can be found in oriental food shops.

**Fontina**
An Italian cow's-milk cheese from the high alpine meadows of the Valle d'Aosta, Fontina is pale and creamy, with a deep rust-brown rind and a delicate nutty flavor, and it melts well when heated. Fontina is available from Italian food stores and good cheese suppliers. Mozzarella can be used as an alternative.

**Garbanzo-bean flour**
Also called besan or gram flour, this finely milled, pale yellow flour is made from roasted garbanzo beans. It is used extensively in Indian cooking and is also used in French, North African, and Middle Eastern dishes.

**Kefalotyri**
This is a strongly flavored Greek sheep's-milk cheese (although occasionally made from goat's milk). It has a sharp, slightly acidic flavor and is mostly used grated in cooked dishes. Pecorino Sardo makes a good alternative.

**Lime leaves**
Aromatic lime leaves from the kaffir lime are widely used in Thai and Indonesian cooking. Lime leaves are available from some supermarkets and oriental food stores. Lime zest can be substituted.

**Pancetta**
An Italian bacon, pancetta is sold both smoked and unsmoked. Other bacon can be used as an alternative.

**Pasta flour**
This highly graded extra-fine wheat flour is used to make pasta dough. Available from Italian food stores and some supermarkets.

**Pecorino Sardo**
Pecorino, an Italian hard cheese, is the Italian generic term for ewe's-milk cheese. Pecorino Sardo is made in Sardinia, and is similar to Parmesan in both flavor and texture.

**Pimento**
Pimentos are sweet red Spanish peppers, available dried or in cans.

**Plantain**
Indigenous to the Caribbean, and Central and South America, the plantain is a vegetable that actually belongs to the banana family. It is much blander and starchier than the banana, and needs cooking to bring out its flavor. Buy ripe plantains, which will have turned from green to yellow to black while ripening.

### Prosecco
Prosecco is is a very light and delicate Italian sparkling wine. A cava or *methode champenoise* may be substituted.

### Reblochon
A semi-soft French mountain cheese with a deep yellow rind, Reblochon is shaped in small rounds and set on wooden disks. It has a wonderful deep fruity flavor and cooks well. Camembert or Brie can be used instead.

### Rice vinegar
Made from fermented rice wine, this vinegar is used extensively in Far Eastern cooking. Sherry vinegar can be used as an alternative.

### Salt cod
This is cod that has been gutted and cleaned and then soaked in brine, preserved in salt, and dried. It is principally from the Scandinavian countries, although it is prepared throughout the Mediterranean. It needs to be soaked for at least 24 hours before cooking.

### Serrano ham
This thinly sliced ham is similar to *Prosciutto di Parma* but comes from Serrano in Spain.

### Smoked mozzarella
As the name suggests, this is simply mozzarella cheese that has been smoked. It is not readily available, although good cheese suppliers and some Italian delicatessens may stock it.

### Tahini
Tahini is a paste made from grinding roasted sesame seeds. It is sold in jars and will separate with age, so stir well before use. Tahini is available in Middle Eastern stores and large supermarkets.

### Thai fish sauce
Thai fish sauce, also known as *nam pla*, is the salt of Thai cooking. It is made from fermented fish and is used extensively in Thai dishes. Use light soy sauce as an alternative.

### Vermicelli rice noodles
Made from rice, these thin noodles are a staple of the diet in southern China. They are used in soups as well as in meat, fish, and vegetable dishes. Follow the instructions on the package for soaking.

### Zucchini flowers
The flowers of the zucchini plant are rarely seen in markets or used in cooking here, unless you are fortunate enough to grow your own. Zucchini flowers are far more common in the Mediterranean countries, where they are stuffed and baked as well as dipped in batter and deep-fried.

## SEAFOOD PREPARATION

Some of the recipes in this book require prepared fresh seafood. Follow these simple instructions if preparing it yourself.

### Cooked crab
Twist off the claws and legs of the crab, then crack open, pick out, and reserve the meat. Holding the shell in your hands, press down firmly against the tail section until it breaks away. Pull out and discard the innards and gills found just behind the mouth, and the feathery beards either side of the body. Scrape out the dark shell meat and pick out the white meat from the body cavity.

### Fresh mussels
Scrub well to remove any mud and tiny shells attached to the mussels. Pull out the scraggly beards that often remain hanging from the closed shell. Tap the mussels gently and discard any that remain open, as they are dead.

### Fresh oysters
Ask your fishmonger to shuck (open) the oysters for you. Carefully snip the muscle that attaches them to their shell.

### Fresh scallops
If the scallops are still in their shells, ask your fishmonger to clean them for you. Take the shelled scallop and cut away the protruding tough muscle from each one and remove the dark vein. Wash and dry well.

### Raw shrimp
Cut off the head, if supplied, and peel away the shells and legs. Cut along the back of each shrimp with a sharp knife and pull out the black vein, the intestine. Wash and dry well.

### Squid
Hold the squid body gently in one hand and the tentacles in the other. Pull the tentacles away from the sac gently but firmly. Most of the squid innards should come out too and should be discarded. Cut off the tentacles and reserve, discarding the sharp beak. You should now be able to peel away the skin easily,. Pull out the transparent quill-like cartilage from the back of each squid, and wash out the sac. Cut the sac into thin rings, and dry well by patting gently all over with paper towels.

Clockwise from far left: Caraway Crackers; Garlic, Chive Sables; and Spicy Palmiers

Serve your guests a selection of the following morsels as you pass around pre-dinner drinks. Spike the Marinated Olives, Chorizo Sausage with Bread, and the Pork, Prosciutto, and Sage Rolls with toothpicks for easy serving.

# one bite

Makes: 24
**Preparation time:** 10 minutes
**Cooking time:** 15 minutes

# spicy palmiers

*Both variations of this recipe make a tasty pre-dinner snack.*

½ x 17¼ oz package frozen puff pastry, thawed

2 tablespoons olive oil

½ teaspoon paprika

pinch of ground cayenne pepper

3 tablespoons freshly grated Parmesan cheese

- Roll out the puff pastry thinly on a lightly floured surface and trim to make a 8 x 10-inch rectangle.
- Combine the oil, paprika, cayenne, and Parmesan, and brush three-quarters of the paste all over the pastry to give an even coating.
- Fold both long sides of pastry in to meet in the middle, spread over a layer of the remaining paste, and fold the pastry in half lengthwise. Press down firmly.
- Preheat the oven to 400°F. Using a sharp knife, cut the pastry into 24 thin slices and transfer, cut side down, to 2 greased baking sheets.
- Bake for 10 minutes, turn over, and bake for a further 4–5 minutes, until the pastries are crisp and golden. Cool on a wire rack. These are best eaten the same day.

## *variation*
## anchovy palmiers

½ x 17¼-oz package frozen puff pastry, thawed

2 tablespoons Anchoïade (see page 124)

- Follow the method above but replace the filling with the Anchoïade.

**Preparation time:** 10 minutes
**Cooking time:** 15 minutes

Makes: 28–30
**Preparation time:** 5 minutes, plus chilling time
**Cooking time:** 15 minutes

# garlic, chive *sables*

- Sift the flour and salt into a bowl and rub in the butter until the mixture resembles fine bread crumbs.
- Work in the cream cheese, garlic, chives, and 1–2 tablespoons of cold water to form a soft dough. Knead lightly, wrap in plastic wrap, and chill for 30 minutes.
- Preheat the oven to 400°F. Roll the pastry out thinly on a lightly floured surface and, using a 2½-inch pastry cutter, stamp out rounds. Re-roll the pastry trimmings and repeat to make 28–30 rounds. Transfer to 2 baking sheets.
- Brush lightly with the beaten egg and bake for 15 minutes, until golden. Cool on a wire rack. These are best when eaten the same day.

1½ cups all-purpose flour
a pinch of salt
⅓ cup butter, diced
2 tablespoons cream cheese
1 garlic clove, crushed
2 tablespoon chopped fresh
  chives
1 small egg, beaten

# caraway crackers

*Serve these crackers as a nibble with an aperitif, or with cheese. Fennel seeds can be substituted for the caraway seeds, if liked.*

- Sift the flour, salt, and cumin into a bowl. Rub in the butter until the mixture resembles fine bread crumbs.
- Stir in the caraway seeds and then gradually work in 2–3 tablespoons water to form a soft dough.
- Knead lightly until smooth, cover with plastic wrap, and rest for 30 minutes.
- Preheat the oven to 375°F. Roll the dough out thinly on a lightly floured surface and, using a 3-inch pastry cutter, stamp out rounds. Re-roll once and repeat to make 16–18 rounds.
- Transfer the crackers to a large baking sheet, prick the surfaces with a fork, and bake for 10 minutes. Turn the crackers over and bake for a further 5 minutes, until crisp and lightly golden. Cool on a wire rack and store in an airtight container for up to 2 days.

1 cup all-purpose flour
¼ teaspoon salt
½ teaspoon ground cumin
¼ cup butter, diced
1–2 teaspoons caraway seeds,
  according to taste

Makes: 16–18
**Preparation time:** 15–20 minutes, plus resting time
**Cooking time:** 15 minutes

1½ cups large whole green
  olives
2 garlic cloves, sliced
grated zest ½ lemon
1 tablespoon balsamic vinegar
½ teaspoon chile flakes
¼ cup extra-virgin olive oil

# marinated olives

○ Place the olives in a bowl, add the remaining ingredients, and stir well. Cover and refrigerate for up to 3 days.

Serves: 8
**Preparation time:** 5 minutes

1½ cups mixed whole green
  and black olives
1 garlic clove, crushed
1 teaspoon grated ginger
2 lime leaves, shredded or
  grated zest 1 lime
2 red chiles, bruised
2 tablespoons dark soy sauce
extra-virgin olive oil, to cover

*variation*
## olives marinated with Asian flavors

○ Place all the ingredients in a bowl and stir well. Cover and refrigerate for up to 1 week.

Serves: 8
**Preparation time:** 5 minutes

# salted almonds

- Heat the oil in a small, heavy-based skillet, add the nuts in several batches, and stir-fry over a medium heat until evenly browned.
- Using a slotted spoon, transfer the nuts to a bowl and add plenty of sea salt. Stir to coat the nuts. Store in an airtight container for up to 3 days.

6 tablespoons olive oil
1½ cups blanched almonds
sea salt

Serves: 4
**Preparation time**: 2 minutes
**Cooking time:** 5 minutes

## *variation*
## spicy glazed cashews

- Melt the butter in a small, heavy-based skillet and then stir in the honey, salt, and cayenne with 1 tablespoon of water. Bring to a boil.
- Add the cashew nuts and stir over a medium heat for 5 minutes until the nuts are toasted and well coated with the glaze. Tip out onto a greased baking sheet and leave to cool. These are best eaten the same day.

2 tablespoons unsalted butter
3 tablespoons clear honey
1 teaspoon salt
¼ teaspoon cayenne pepper
1½ cups cashew nuts

Serves: 8
**Preparation time:** 3 minutes
**Cooking time:** 6–7 minutes

Makes: approximately 12 falafel
**Preparation time:** 10 minutes, plus overnight soaking and chilling time
**Cooking time:** 6–8 minutes

¾ cup dried fava beans,
   soaked overnight in cold
   water
2 tablespoons yogurt
1 tablespoon tahini paste
1 tablespoon lemon juice
1 garlic clove, crushed
1 teaspoon ground coriander
½ teaspoon ground cumin
½ teaspoon cayenne pepper
1 tablespoon chopped fresh
   cilantro
1 tablespoon chopped fresh
   mint
salt and pepper
vegetable oil, for shallow-frying
yogurt, to serve

# falafel

*These patties are a traditional Middle Eastern snack. The mixture is quite wet and crumbly when you come to shape them, but this ensures a perfect, light texture when they are fried.*

- Drain the fava beans and dry thoroughly. Place in a food processor and blend to form a fairly smooth paste. Transfer the purée to a bowl. Stir in all the remaining ingredients, season with salt and pepper, cover, and chill for 1 hour.
- Form the mixture into small patties. Heat a shallow layer of oil in a non-stick skillet and fry the patties a few at a time for 1–2 minutes on each side, until golden. Serve with yogurt.

# root
## *vegetable chips*

*These tasty chips are easy to make at home, so of course you can use your favorite root vegetables.*

2 beets
1 large potato
1 small sweet potato
2 carrots
2 parsnips
vegetable oil, for deep-frying
sea salt
cayenne pepper (optional)

- Slice the vegetables into fine wafers using a potato peeler or mandoline, keeping them in separate batches. (It is best to cut the carrots and parsnips lengthwise.)
- Heat 2 inches vegetable oil in a deep saucepan until it reaches 350–375°F, or until a cube of bread browns in 30 seconds. Pat the vegetables dry using paper towels.
- Again, keeping the vegetables separate, deep-fry them in batches for 30 seconds to 1½ minutes, until crisp and golden. Drain on paper towels and leave to cool on a wire rack.
- Transfer the chips to a large bowl and sprinkle with sea salt and a little cayenne, if using. Pass the chips around in small bowls.

Serves: 2–4
**Preparation time:** 10 minutes
**Cooking time:** 8–10 minutes

1 teaspoon fennel seeds

1 teaspoon pink peppercorns

8 oz goat cheese, such as
Sainte Maure

2 garlic cloves, peeled but left
whole

2 small green chiles, bruised

2 sprigs fresh rosemary,
bruised

2 bay leaves, bruised

extra-virgin olive oil, to cover

crusty French bread, to serve

Serves: 8
**Preparation time:** 15 minutes

# marinated
*goat cheese*

*The herbs and spices added to the oil infuse the goat cheese as it marinates, giving it a wonderful delicate flavor.*

- Put the fennel seeds and peppercorns in a small, heavy-based skillet and heat gently until they start to pop and release an aroma. Leave to cool completely.
- Roll the cheese into small balls and place in a bowl or jar. Add the cooled fennel seeds and peppercorns, then add the remaining ingredients with sufficient olive oil to cover.
- Store in a cool place for at least 3 days, but no longer than 1 week. Serve the cheese balls with a little of the oil and chunks of French bread, or spread on slices of toasted French bread.

# *deep-fried*
# artichokes

*You do not have to use baby artichokes for this dish. If they are not available or you want to use larger artichokes, steam or boil them before deep-frying them.*

12 baby artichokes

1 lemon, halved

vegetable oil, for deep-frying

¼ cup flour, seasoned with salt and pepper

salt, to serve

lemon wedges, to garnish

○ Trim the artichokes and cut each one lengthwise in half or quarters, depending on the size. Rub all over the cut surface with the halved lemon.

○ Heat 2 inches vegetable oil in a deep skillet until it reaches 350–375°F, or until a cube of bread browns in 30 seconds.

○ Dip the artichokes in the seasoned flour to coat well and deep-fry in batches for 1–2 minutes, until crisp and golden. Drain on paper towels. Serve sprinkled with salt and garnished with lemon wedges.

Serves: 4
**Preparation time:** 20 minutes
**Cooking time:** 1–2 minutes each batch

# *deep-fried*
# onion rings
# in beer batter

*These are far superior to any frozen onion rings you can buy, and are definitely worth making yourself.*

○ Slice the onions into ¼-inch thick rings and separate. Reserve all the larger rings and put the rest aside for use in another dish.

○ In a bowl, beat the egg yolk, oil, and beer with the flour, and season to taste with salt and pepper. In another bowl, whisk the egg white until stiff and fold into the batter until evenly incorporated.

○ Heat 2 inches vegetable oil in a deep saucepan until it reaches 350–375°F, or until a cube of bread browns in 30 seconds. Dip the onion rings, a few at a time, into the batter, then deep-fry for 1–2 minutes, until golden. Remove with a slotted spoon and drain on paper towels.

○ Serve the onion rings hot with a bowl of Mayonnaise or Aïoli, to dip.

4 large onions
vegetable oil, for deep-frying
Mayonnaise or Aïoli, to serve
  (see page 125)

**Batter:**
1 egg, separated
1 tablespoon olive oil
7 tablespoons light beer
9 tablespoons all-purpose flour
salt and pepper

Serves: 4–6
**Preparation time:** 10 minutes
**Cooking time:** 10 minutes

# *deep-fried* mozzarella balls

*If you cannot find any mozzarella balls, which are known as boconcinni, buy a whole mozzarella and cut it into bite-sized chunks.*

- Dry the mozzarella balls thoroughly using paper towels, then dip first in the seasoned flour, then the egg, and finally the bread crumbs. Chill for 30 minutes.
- Heat 2 inches vegetable oil in a deep saucepan until it reaches 350–375°F, or until a cube of bread browns in 30 seconds. Deep-fry the mozzarella balls, in batches for 30 seconds to 1 minute, until crisp and golden. Remove with a slotted spoon and drain on paper towels. Keep warm in the oven while cooking the remainder.
- Serve at once with the Smoky Tomato Salsa.

12 mozzarella balls
  (boconcinni)
2 tablespoons flour, seasoned
  with salt and pepper
1 egg, beaten
¼ cup dried bread crumbs
vegetable oil, for deep-frying
1 recipe Smoky Tomato Salsa,
  to serve (see page 118)

Serves: 4
**Preparation time:** 5 minutes, plus chilling time
**Cooking time:** 30 seconds to 1 minute each

# lamb and zucchini koftas

*Delicious served with a sweet relish or even redcurrant jelly.*

- Place the finely grated zucchini in a strainer and press down to extract as much liquid as possible. Place in a bowl.
- Dry-fry the sesame seeds in a skillet for 1–2 minutes until they are golden and release their aroma. Add to the zucchini, then add the lamb and all the remaining ingredients except the oil and lemon. Season liberally with salt and pepper.
- Form the mixture into 20 small balls and shallow-fry in batches for 5 minutes, turning frequently until evenly browned. Keep the koftas warm in a hot oven while cooking the rest. Serve hot, garnished with lemon wedges.

2 zucchini, finely grated
2 tablespoons sesame seeds
1 cup ground lamb
2 scallions, finely chopped
1 garlic clove, crushed
1 tablespoon chopped fresh
  mint
½ teaspoon ground mixed
  spice
2 tablespoons dried bread
  crumbs
1 egg, lightly beaten
salt and pepper
vegetable oil, for shallow-frying
lemon wedges, to garnish

Serves: 4
**Preparation time:** 20 minutes
**Cooking time:** 5 minutes each batch

1 egg, separated

1 tablespoon olive oil

7 tablespoons Prosecco or
sparkling mineral water

9 tablespoons all-purpose
flour

vegetable oil, for deep-frying

small bunch of mixed fresh
herb sprigs, to include flat-
leaf parsley, basil, cilantro,
mint, and sage

salt and pepper

salt, to serve

lemon wedges, to garnish

Serves: 4–6
**Preparation time**: 5 minutes
**Cooking time:** 30 seconds each

# herb fritters

*These batter-coated herb sprigs become mouthwateringly tender and succulent as they cook. Try to avoid using rosemary and thyme with very tough stalks. Prosecco is an Italian sparking wine that adds a delicate flavor to the batter. Sparkling mineral water can be used instead.*

- In a bowl, beat the egg yolk, oil, and Prosecco or mineral water with the flour, and season with salt and pepper. In another bowl, whisk the egg white until stiff, then fold into the batter until evenly incorporated.
- Heat 2 inches vegetable oil in a deep saucepan until it reaches 350–375°F, or until a cube of bread browns in 30 seconds.
- Taking only a few herbs at a time, dip the sprigs into the batter and deep-fry for 30 seconds, until crisp and golden. Drain on paper towels and keep warm in a hot oven while cooking the remaining fritters.
- Serve hot sprinkled with salt and garnished with lemon wedges to squeeze over.

⅓ cup golden raisins
4 tablespoons Marsala
4 pork scallops
4 slices prosciutto
16 large sage leaves
4 oz Fontina cheese, without rind, cut into wafer thin slices
salt and pepper
olive oil, for shallow-frying
1 recipe Salsa Verde, to serve (see page 120)

Serves: 8
**Preparation time:** 20 minutes, plus soaking time
**Cooking time:** 10 minutes

# pork, prosciutto, and sage rolls
## *with salsa verde*

*Fontina is an Italian semi-soft cow's-milk cheese with a nutty flavor. It melts easily and is similar to mozzarella cheese, which may be used as a substitute.*

- Mix the golden raisins with the Marsala and set aside to macerate for 1 hour. Drain and pat the raisins dry.
- Place each pork scallop between 2 pieces of parchment paper and pound flat with a mallet or rolling pin. Trim the scallop to an approximate rectangle.
- Top each scallop with a slice of prosciutto, 4 sage leaves, a quarter of the cheese, and a quarter of the golden raisins. Season with salt and pepper.
- Roll up the scallops from one long side and skewer with wooden toothpicks to secure. Heat a little oil in a skillet and fry the pork rolls for 10 minutes over a medium heat until browned all over.
- Remove the pork rolls from the skillet and leave to cool to room temperature. Remove and discard the toothpicks and slice each roll into bite-sized pieces. Spear with clean toothpicks and serve with the Salsa Verde.

# spicy crab and chicken purses

## *with sweet and sour dipping sauce*

*Here squares of phyllo pastry are stuffed with a Chinese-style chicken and crab filling and baked until crisp and golden. The dipping sauce adds a lovely sweet contrast.*

- Place all the ingredients except the phyllo pastry and oil in a bowl and stir well until combined. Cover and chill for 1 hour to allow the flavors to develop.
- Meanwhile, prepare the dipping sauce. Place all the ingredients in a small saucepan and heat gently, stirring until the sugar is dissolved. Bring to a boil and remove from the heat. Leave until cold and transfer to a small serving bowl.
- Preheat the oven to 375°F. Cut the phyllo pastry into 5-inch squares. Brush each one with oil and place a spoonful of the crab and chicken mixture in the center. Draw the edges up to a point and pinch together. Place the purses on a large greased baking sheet, brush them with oil, and bake for 20–25 minutes, until golden and crisp.
- Serve the purses hot with the dipping sauce.

Makes: 24
**Preparation time:** 10 minutes, plus chilling time
**Cooking time:** 20–25 minutes

¾ cup white crab meat, drained if canned
¾ cup cooked chicken, minced
1 garlic clove, crushed
2 scallions, chopped
1 tablespoon fresh cilantro, chopped
2 teaspoons chopped preserved ginger, plus 2 teaspoons ginger syrup from the jar
¼ teaspoon chile powder
1 tablespoon light soy sauce
grated zest and juice 1 lime
4 phyllo pastry sheets, thawed if frozen
¼ cup olive oil, plus extra for greasing and brushing

**Sweet and Sour Dipping Sauce:**

¼ cup sugar
3 tablespoons rice or wine vinegar
½ teaspoon salt
1 teaspoon dried chile flakes
2 tablespoons water

Serves: 4
**Preparation time:** 5 minutes
**Cooking time:** 5 minutes

# chorizo sausage
## *with bread*

8-oz piece mild chorizo
  sausage
3 tablespoons extra-virgin
  olive oil
1 garlic clove, sliced
¼ teaspoon dried chile flakes
2 slices country bread, cubed

- Cut the sausage into ¼-inch-thick slices. Heat the oil in a small skillet, add the garlic and chile flakes, and fry gently for 30 seconds to 1 minute, until they release their aroma. Do not allow them to burn.
- Strain the oil and return to the skillet. Add the sausage and stir-fry for 1–2 minutes, until golden. Remove with a slotted spoon.
- Toss the bread cubes briefly in the pan juices and drain. Spear a slice of sausage and cube of bread together on toothpicks and serve warm.

# salt cod *fritters*

8 oz salt cod
⅔ cup milk
8 oz potatoes, cubed
1 garlic clove, crushed
2 scallions, finely chopped
1 tablespoon chopped fresh
  cilantro
1 egg yolk
pepper
vegetable oil, for shallow-frying

**To Serve:**
Skordalia (see page 121) or
  Mayonnaise (see page 125)
lemon wedges

- Put the salt cod into a bowl and cover with cold water. Leave to soak for 24 hours, changing the water several times.
- The next day drain the fish and dry well. Remove the skin and bones, and cut the fish into small cubes. Place in a bowl, cover with the milk, and leave for 2 hours.
- Drain the cod and place in a saucepan with the potatoes. Cover with water, bring to a boil, and simmer, covered, for 20 minutes, until tender.
- Drain and mash the fish and potatoes together. Beat in the remaining ingredients, except for the oil, and season with pepper.
- Heat about 1 inch of oil in a deep skillet. Drop teaspoons of the cod mixture into the oil. Fry for 1–2 minutes, until the fritters are browned on all sides.
- Drain on paper towels and keep warm in a hot oven while frying the remaining fritters. Serve hot with Skordalia or Mayonnaise to dip, and lemon wedges to squeeze over.

Serves: 8
**Preparation time:** 35 minutes, plus soaking time
**Cooking time:** 1–2 minutes each batch

20 large fresh mussels

1 cup fresh basil leaves

1 garlic clove, crushed

1 small red chile, seeded and diced

½ teaspoon grated lemon zest

1 tablespoon pine nuts

1 tablespoon freshly grated Parmesan
   cheese

2 tablespoon fresh bread crumbs

3–4 tablespoons extra-virgin olive oil

salt and pepper

# broiled mussels

- Wash and scrub the mussels, pulling out any scraggly beard still attached to the shells. Steam the mussels with just the water on their shells for 4 minutes, until they have just opened. Discard any that do not open. Immediately plunge the mussels into cold water, then drain again.
- Carefully discard one half of each shell. Arrange the mussels in their shells in 1 large dish or 4 individual gratin dishes.
- In a blender or food processor combine the basil, garlic, chile, lemon zest, pine nuts, Parmesan, and half of the bread crumbs. Pulse briefly to form a smooth paste and season to taste with salt and pepper.
- Preheat the broiler. Transfer the basil paste to a bowl and stir in the oil. Spoon a little of the paste over each mussel and top each one with a few more bread crumbs. Broil for 2–3 minutes, until bubbling and golden. Serve at once.

Serves: 4
**Preparation time:** 15 minutes
**Cooking time:** 2–3 minutes

Several of the recipes in this chapter benefit from cooking over charcoal, particularly the Broiled Corn with Flavored Butters, Chicken Saté, and Broiled Sweet Potatoes with Cilantro and Lemon Salsa. So why not get the barbecue out as soon as the sun arrives?

# two bites

# cheese-stuffed
# phyllo fingers

Makes: 20
**Preparation time:** 25 minutes
**Cooking time:** 15–20 minutes

8 oz Kefalotyri cheese, finely
grated
8 oz ricotta cheese
2 eggs, lightly beaten
2 tablespoons chopped fresh
mint
6 sheets phyllo pastry
olive oil
2 tablespoons sesame seeds
pepper

*Kefalotyri is a hard sheep's-milk cheese from Greece. The crumbly texture, pale color and salty flavor resemble the Sardinian sheep's-milk cheese, Pecorino Sardo, which makes a suitable alternative.*

- In a bowl beat the cheeses with the eggs and mint, and season with black pepper.
- Trim the phyllo pastry sheets to 8 x 10 inches, if necessary. Then cut each sheet in half lengthwise and then crosswise to make 24 pieces.
- Working with 1 piece of pastry at a time (keeping the rest covered with a slightly damp dish towel), brush the pastry with oil.
- Preheat the oven to 400°F. Place a little of the filling along one long side of the pastry and roll up to enclose the filling. Repeat to make 24 fingers. Place on a lightly oiled large baking sheet.
- Brush the fingers with oil and sprinkle with sesame seeds. Bake for 15–20 minutes, until golden. Serve at once.

# deep-fried
# calamari

Serves: 4
**Preparation time:** 15 minutes
**Cooking time:** 1–2 minutes each batch

1 lb small squid, cleaned
vegetable oil, for deep-frying
2 eggs, lightly beaten
2–4 tablespoons flour,
seasoned with salt, pepper
and a pinch cayenne pepper

**To Serve:**
sea salt
lemon juice
1 recipe Aïoli (see page 125)

- Cut the squid into rings and halve the tentacles, if large. Wash well and dry thoroughly on paper towels.
- Heat 2 inches vegetable oil in a deep saucepan until it reaches 350–375°F, or until a cube of bread browns in 30 seconds.
- Meanwhile dip the squid into the beaten egg and coat with the seasoned flour. Deep-fry in batches for 1–2 minutes, until crisp and golden. Drain each batch on paper towels.
- Keep the cooked squid warm in a hot oven while cooking the remainder. Serve hot sprinkled with sea salt, drizzled with lemon juice, and accompanied by a bowl of Aïoli to dip.

1 tablespoon butter

½ teaspoon sea salt

6 tablespoons quick cooking polenta

2 tablespoons freshly grated Parmesan cheese

6 oz mozzarella cheese

18 large basil leaves

¼ cup flour, seasoned with salt and pepper

2 eggs, beaten

½ cup dried plain white bread crumbs

vegetable oil, for deep-frying

pepper

Serves: 8

**Preparation time:** 20 minutes, plus setting and chilling time

**Cooking time:** 1–2 minutes each batch

# polenta triangle sandwiches

*These are triangles of set polenta, sandwiched together with mozzarella cheese. They are then coated in bread crumbs and deep-fried. The mozzarella melts and starts to ooze as it cooks, making a rich and delicious morsel.*

- Grease an 8 x 12 inch pan. Bring 1 quart water to a rolling boil, add the butter and salt, and then gradually whisk in the polenta in a steady stream.
- Simmer over a low heat for 5–6 minutes, stirring constantly until the mixture comes away from the sides of the pan. Stir in the Parmesan, season with black pepper, and pour into the prepared pan. Smooth the surface and set aside to cool.
- Turn the set polenta out and trim to a 6-inch square. Cut into 2-inch squares and then cut each square in half diagonally to make 18 triangles. Cut the mozzarella into thin slices and then into triangles roughly the same size as the polenta.
- Place a triangular slice of mozzarella over half the polenta triangles, top with a basil leaf and a piece of polenta.
- Dip the polenta sandwiches in the seasoned flour, then into the beaten egg and finally in the bread crumbs to coat well. Chill for 1 hour.
- Heat 2 inches vegetable oil in a deep saucepan until it reaches 350–375°F, or until a cube of bread browns in 30 seconds.
- Deep-fry the triangles in batches for 1–2 minutes, until crisp and golden. Drain on paper towels and keep warm in a hot oven while frying the rest. Serve hot.

Serves: 4
**Preparation time:** 10 minutes
**Cooking time:** 6–8 minutes

# broiled sweet potatoes

*with cilantro and lemon salsa*

1 lb sweet potatoes
¼ cup olive oil
2 garlic cloves, crushed
salt and pepper

**Cilantro and
Lemon Salsa:**

¼ cup chopped cilantro
1 small red chile, seeded and
   finely chopped
1 small garlic clove, crushed
6 tablespoons extra-virgin
   olive oil
grated zest and juice of 1
   lemon
½–1 teaspoon ground cumin

○ Scrub the sweet potatoes well but do not peel them. Cut into ¼-inch-thick slices, pat dry on paper towels, and place in a large bowl.

○ Mix the olive oil and garlic, and season well with salt and pepper. Pour over the sweet potato slices and toss well to coat.

○ Preheat the broiler. Arrange the potato slices in a single layer on a rack placed over the broiler pan. Broil for 6–8 minutes on each side or until charred and cooked through.

○ Meanwhile, prepare the salsa. Combine all the ingredients in a bowl and season to taste with salt and pepper. Transfer the cooked sweet potato slices to a plate, spoon over the salsa, and serve at once.

Serves: 2–4
**Preparation time:** 18–20 minutes, plus soaking and marinating time
**Cooking time:** 4–5 minutes

# Thai-style
## *spicy mushroom skewers*

*You can buy dried shiitake mushrooms from oriental stores, where you might find a wide variety of larger shiitake mushrooms. Alternatively, you could dry your own: buy large fresh shiitake and leave them to dry on newspaper for 2–3 days in a warm, dry place, then use as required. This recipe is inspired by a dish cooked by Thai chef Vatcherin Bhumichitr in his restaurant, Chang Mai.*

- Put the dried mushrooms into a bowl and pour over enough boiling water to cover. Leave to soak for 2 hours. Drain the mushrooms and dry thoroughly on paper towels. Cut away the tough stalks.
- Using small scissors, cut each mushroom into one long spiral strip starting from the outside and following the shape to the middle.
- Thread the mushroom strips onto bamboo skewers that have been soaked in cold water for 30 minutes, weaving the mushrooms back and forth to zigzag along the skewers.
- Blend the coriander, garlic, pepper, and salt, and stir in the sunflower oil and lemon juice. Spread this mixture all over the mushrooms, cover, and leave to marinate for at least 1 hour.
- Preheat the broiler. Place the mushroom skewers on a rack set over a broiler pan, and brush with a little oil. Broil for 4–5 minutes, turning once, until the mushrooms are charred and tender. Serve at once with the Saté Sauce to dip.

16 large dried shiitake mushrooms
2 teaspoons freshly ground coriander
1 garlic clove, crushed
½ teaspoon ground black pepper
½ teaspoon salt
2 tablespoons sunflower oil, plus extra for brushing
2 teaspoons lemon juice
1 recipe Saté Sauce, to serve (see page 50)

Serves: 8
**Preparation time:** 45 minutes
**Cooking time:** 1–2 minutes each batch

# shrimp, rice, and pea croquettes

*Traditionally, these small rice patties were made from leftover paella. However, they are so delicious that they have become a dish in their own right.*

1 tablespoon butter

1 garlic clove, crushed

2 shallots, finely chopped

⅓ cup arborio rice

2⅔ cups fish or vegetable stock

½ cup cooked, peeled shrimp, roughly chopped

1 cup frozen peas

2 tablespoons chopped fresh mint

2 tablespoons freshly grated Parmesan cheese

2 eggs, beaten

2–4 tablespoons flour, seasoned with salt and pepper

1 cup fresh white bread crumbs

vegetable oil, for deep-frying

salt and pepper

○ Melt the butter in a small saucepan and fry the garlic and shallots for 5 minutes. Add the rice and stir-fry for 30 seconds to coat all the grains.

○ Add a ladleful of the stock and simmer until reduced. Continue adding stock and stirring the rice for 20 minutes.

○ With the final ladle of stock add the shrimp and peas, cover, and cook for 5–10 minutes, until the rice is *al dente* and the peas are cooked.

○ Remove the pot from the heat, stir in the chopped mint and grated Parmesan, and season to taste with salt and pepper. Cover the surface with waxed paper and set aside to cool.

○ Once the mixture is cool, beat in half the beaten eggs, 2 tablespoons of seasoned flour, and 3 tablespoons of the bread crumbs. Form into 2-inch flat patties, dust with seasoned flour, dip into the remaining beaten egg, and coat with the remaining bread crumbs.

○ Heat 2 inches of oil in a deep saucepan until it reaches 350–375°F, or until a cube of bread browns in 30 seconds.

○ Deep-fry the patties in batches for 1–2 minutes, until golden, then drain on paper towels, and keep warm in a hot oven while frying the remaining croquettes. Serve at once.

3 small ears corn

**Fennel and Thyme Butter:**

1 teaspoon fennel seeds

¼ cup unsalted butter, softened

1 teaspoon chopped fresh thyme

½ teaspoon finely grated lemon zest

1 small garlic clove, crushed

salt and pepper

**Chile and Lime Butter with Sesame:**

1 tablespoon sesame seeds

¼ cup unsalted butter, softened

1 small red chile, seeded and finely chopped

grated zest and juice ½–1 lime

Serves: 6

**Preparation time:** 15 minutes, plus chilling time

**Cooking time:** 10–12 minutes

# broiled corn
## *with flavored butters*

*Use a mallet to help cut through the corn cobs, which tend to be very tough.*

- Start by making the 2 butters. Dry-fry the fennel seeds in a small saucepan until they start to pop and release their aroma. Cool slightly and blend in a spice grinder to form a rough powder.

- Place all the remaining Fennel and Thyme Butter ingredients in a food processor, add the ground fennel, and blend until combined. Season to taste with salt and pepper. Transfer the butter to a piece of foil and roll into a sausage shape. Chill for 30 minutes.

- To make the Chile and Lime Butter, dry-fry the sesame seeds in a small saucepan until golden. Allow the sesame seeds to cool slightly, then place in a food processor with all the remaining ingredients. Season to taste with salt and pepper. Process until combined. Roll and chill as with the Fennel and Thyme Butter.

- Using a large sharp knife, cut the corn into ½-inch-thick slices and arrange on a rack set over a broiler pan.

- Preheat the broiler. Remove both butters from their foil and cut into thin slices. Top half the corn slices with one butter and the other half with the remaining butter. Place a good few inches below the heat source, and broil for about 10–12 minutes, turning and adding more butter as required until golden and tender. Serve at once.

2 tablespoons olive oil, plus extra for greasing

2 cups garbanzo-bean flour

Chile Oil, for shallow-frying (see page 119)

sea salt and pepper

Serves: 12
**Preparation time:** 10 minutes, plus setting time
**Cooking time:** 2–4 minutes

# chile-fried panisse

*Panisse originates from Nice and is similar to Socca, which is a street food common to Provence, but Socca is sweet and Panisse savory. Traditionally, the fingers are deep-fried, but here I shallow fry them in chile oil.*

- Oil a 9 x 4-inch roasting pan. Sift the flour into a bowl and stir in 1 teaspoon of sea salt. Bring 4½ cups water to a rolling boil. Add the olive oil to the bowl and then gradually whisk in the water until smooth. Transfer to a non-stick saucepan.

- Bring the mixture to a boil, stirring constantly, and cook for 5–6 minutes, until thickened and smooth. Transfer the mixture to the prepared pan and leave to cool.

- Turn out of the pan and cut the panisse into fingers. Heat some Chile Oil in a non-stick skillet and fry the fingers for 1–2 minutes on each side, until golden.

- Season with salt and pepper and serve hot.

Serves: 6
**Preparation time:** 15 minutes
**Cooking time:** 1–2 minutes each batch

# shrimp puffs

12 large raw tiger shrimp
vegetable oil, for deep-frying
2 eggs
2 large scallions, trimmed and
  finely chopped
½ teaspoon Chinese five spice
  powder
2 tablespoons all-purpose
  flour
salt and pepper
1 recipe Dipping Sauce, to
  serve (see page 67)

- Peel the shrimp leaving the tail section intact. Cut down the back of each one and discard the black vein. Wash the shrimp and dry thoroughly on paper towels.
- Using a sharp knife, cut the shrimp into 3 slices as far down as the tail section.
- Heat 2 inches vegetable oil in a deep saucepan until it reaches 350–375°F, or until a cube of bread browns in 30 seconds.
- In a bowl whisk the eggs, scallions, and Chinese five spice powder, and season with a little salt and pepper. Dip the shrimp into the flour and then into the egg mixture.
- Deep-fry the shrimp in batches in the hot oil for 1–2 minutes, until crisp and golden. Drain on paper towels and serve hot with the Dipping Sauce.

# chile chunks

*Use as little or as much chile powder as you like, to coat these oven-roasted potato chile chips.*

4 large, even-sized potatoes
4–6 tablespoons olive oil
½ teaspoon salt
1–2 teaspoons chile powder,
  to taste
sour cream or 1 recipe
  Mayonnaise or Aïoli, to serve
  (see page 125)

- Preheat the oven to 425°F. Cut each potato into 8 wedges and place in a large bowl. Add the oil, salt, and chile powder, and toss until evenly coated.
- Transfer to a baking sheet and roast for 15 minutes. Turn over and cook for a further 15 minutes. Turn once more and cook for a final 25–30 minutes, until crisp and golden.
- Cool slightly and serve with sour cream, Mayonnaise, or Aïoli.

Serves: 4–6
**Preparation time:** 5 minutes
**Cooking time:** 55–60 minutes

Serves: 6
**Preparation time:** 15 minutes
**Cooking time:** 2–3 minutes each batch

# *sesame*
# shrimp toast

1 scallion, roughly chopped

1 garlic clove, crushed

1 teaspoon grated root ginger

½ cup cooked, peeled shrimp, well dried

1 tablespoon cornstarch

1 teaspoon soy sauce

12 thin slices day-old white bread, crusts removed

¼ cup sesame seeds

vegetable oil, for deep-frying

lemon wedges, to serve

- Put the scallion, garlic, and ginger in a blender or food processor with the shrimp, cornstarch and soy sauce, and pulse to form a smooth paste.
- Spread an even layer of paste over one side of the bread. Cut each piece into four triangles and coat with sesame seeds.
- Heat 2 inches vegetable oil in a deep saucepan and heat until it reaches 350–375°F, or until a cube of bread browns in 30 seconds.
- Deep-fry the triangles in batches for 2–3 minutes, until crisp and golden. Drain on paper towels. Serve hot with lemon wedges.

# *jerk-spiced*
# fried plantains

2 large ripe plantains

1 tablespoon Jamaican jerk spices

2 tablespoons olive oil

2 tablespoons butter

juice 1 lime

salt

*Plantains might be available in some Latin or Caribbean markets.*

- Peel the plantains and cut each one in half crosswise. Cut each half into 4 thin slices, then dust with the jerk spices.
- Heat the oil and butter together in a large non-stick skillet. As soon as the butter stops foaming add the plantains and fry over a medium heat for 3–4 minutes on each side, until golden.
- Remove from the skillet and drain on paper towels. Transfer to a dish and drizzle over the lime juice. Season to taste with salt and serve at once.

Serves: 2–4
**Preparation time:** 6–8 minutes
**Cooking time:** 5 minutes

Serves: 4
**Preparation time:** 5 minutes
**Cooking time:** 8–10 minutes

# broiled mushrooms
## *with garlic oil*

5 tablespoons extra-virgin
   olive oil
2 garlic cloves, crushed
grated zest and juice ½ lime
1 small red chile, seeded and
   finely chopped
2 tablespoons chopped fresh
   parsley
12 large flat mushrooms
salt and pepper

*Here the mushrooms are broiled before being dressed with oil, which intensifies the flavor during the cooking process.*

○ In a small bowl, combine all the ingredients except the mushrooms, and season to taste with salt and pepper.

○ Preheat the broiler. Arrange the mushrooms stalk side down on a foil-lined broiler pan and broil as close to the heat as possible for 3–4 minutes, until beginning to moisten.

○ Flip the mushrooms over and cook for a further 4–5 minutes until cooked through. Transfer to a serving plate and pour over the dressing. Leave to cool to room temperature.

12 small oysters, shucked

1 tablespoon red wine vinegar

1 teaspoon Worcestershire sauce

a few drops Tabasco sauce

2 tablespoons butter

1 shallot, finely chopped

1 garlic clove, crushed

⅓ cup finely chopped pancetta or smoked bacon

1 cup fresh white bread crumbs

2 tablespoons freshly grated Parmesan cheese

1 tablespoon chopped fresh parsley

a little olive oil

salt and pepper

Serves: 6
**Preparation time:** 30 minutes
**Cooking time:** 3–4 minutes

# deviled oysters

*Your fishmonger will shuck (open) the oysters for you, but ask him to leave the oysters and juices in their shells.*

- Carefully strain the juices from the oysters into a bowl and stir in the vinegar, Worcestershire sauce, and Tabasco sauce. Cut through the muscle that attaches the oysters to the deep half of the shell, but leave the oysters in the shell. Discard the other half of the shell.
- Melt the butter in a small saucepan and fry the shallot and garlic for 5 minutes. Add the pancetta or bacon and stir-fry for a further 3–4 minutes, until browned.
- Add the bread crumbs, pour in the oyster juice mixture, and boil until the liquid has nearly all evaporated. Remove from the heat and stir in the Parmesan and parsley, and season to taste with salt and pepper. Leave to cool.
- Preheat the broiler. Arrange the oysters in a baking dish and top each one with the bread-crumb mixture. Drizzle over a little olive oil and broil for 3–4 minutes, until bubbling and golden. Serve at once.

1 lb boneless, skinless chicken breasts

1 small onion, finely chopped

2 teaspoons grated fresh ginger

2 garlic cloves, crushed

2 tablespoons lime juice

1 tablespoon dark soy sauce

1 tablespoon garam masala

½ teaspoon salt

**Saté Sauce:**

1 tablespoons groundnut oil

1 garlic clove, crushed

¼ cup crunchy peanut butter

¼ teaspoon dried chile flakes

1 tablespoon dark soy sauce

1 tablespoon lime juice

1 teaspoon clear honey

2 tablespoons coconut cream

Serves: 4–8

**Preparation time:** 20 minutes, plus overnight marinating time

**Cooking time:** 4–6 minutes

# chicken saté

*Soak the bamboo skewers in cold water for 30 minutes before use. This will prevent them from burning in the broiler.*

- Cut the chicken breasts diagonally into very thin strips and place in a shallow dish. Combine the remaining ingredients to make the marinade and pour over the chicken. Stir once, cover, and leave to marinate overnight.
- To make the saté sauce, heat the groundnut oil in a small saucepan and gently fry the garlic for 2–3 minutes, until softened. Stir in the remaining ingredients and heat gently until boiling.
- Preheat the broiler. Drain the chicken and pat dry. Thread the chicken strips onto 8 pre-soaked bamboo skewers, zigzagging as you go. Broil for 2–3 minutes on each side, until charred and cooked through. Serve with the saté sauce, to dip.

24 vine leaves, preserved in brine, drained

¼ cup olive oil

1 onion, finely chopped

2 garlic cloves, crushed

1 cup long grain rice

1 tablespoon tomato paste

2 teaspoons ground coriander

1 teaspoon ground cumin

2 tablespoons chopped fresh dill

1 tablespoon chopped fresh mint

3 tablespoons dried currants

2 tablespoons pine nuts, toasted

¼ cup lemon juice

salt and pepper

Mint and Garlic Sauce, to serve (see page 72)

lemon wedges, to garnish

# dolmades

- Wash and dry the vine leaves and set aside 16 larger leaves. Use the rest to line an 8-inch square baking dish.
- Heat half the oil in a skillet and fry the onion and garlic for 5 minutes. Add the rice, stir once, then add the remaining ingredients, except the lemon juice.
- Lay out the vine leaves, vein side up, and place a spoonful of the filling in the middle of each leaf. Fold the edges around and over the filling, rolling them into a small sausage shape. Repeat to make 16 dolmades.
- Preheat the oven to 350°F. Transfer the dolmades to the prepared dish, pour over the remaining oil, the lemon juice, and enough water to just cover the parcels. Cover with foil and bake for 1 hour.
- Remove from the oven and leave to cool in the dish. Serve warm or cold with Mint and Garlic Sauce and garnished with lemon wedges.

Serves: 8
**Preparation time:** 30 minutes
**Cooking time:** 1 hour

Serves: 4–6
**Preparation time:** 5 minutes
**Cooking time:** 5 minutes

# fried shrimp with garlic butter

12 large raw tiger shrimp

2 tablespoons olive oil

¼ cup butter

1 garlic clove, crushed

1 tablespoon chopped fresh
  basil

juice 1 lemon

salt and pepper

Aïoli, to serve (see page 125)

- Wash and dry the shrimp. Heat the oil and butter together in a large skillet. When the butter stops foaming, add the shrimp and crushed garlic, and stir-fry for 4–5 minutes until the shrimp are pink and golden.
- Remove the skillet from the heat, stir in the basil, and squeeze over plenty of lemon juice. Season to taste with salt and pepper. Spoon the shrimp into small dishes and serve accompanied with a pot of Aïoli and finger bowls.

# stuffed baby squid

12 baby squid, about
  5 inches long, cleaned

5 tablespoons extra-virgin
  olive oil

1 small onion, chopped finely

2 garlic cloves, crushed

1 teaspoon chopped fresh
  sage

grated zest and juice ½ lemon

1 cup fresh white bread
  crumbs

½ x 2-oz can anchovies,
  drained and chopped

2 tablespoons chopped fresh
  parsley

2 tablepsoons pine nuts,
  toasted and chopped

¼ cup dry white wine

pepper

*Do not overstuff the squid, as the filling expands during cooking.*

- Discard the squid tentacles, wash the body cavity of the squid, and pat dry on paper towels.
- Heat 1 tablespoon of the oil in a skillet and fry the onion, garlic, sage, and lemon zest for 5 minutes. Transfer to a bowl and stir in the bread crumbs, anchovies, parsley, pine nuts, lemon juice, and plenty of black pepper.
- Preheat the oven to 450°F. Use the mixture to stuff the squid bodies and secure the tops with wooden toothpicks. Transfer the stuffed squid to a baking dish, drizzle over the wine and remaining oil, and bake for 20 minutes. Serve at once.

Serves: 4–6
**Preparation time:** 25 minutes
**Cooking time:** 20 minutes

Serves: 4– 6
**Preparation time:** 10 minutes
**Cooking time:** 3 minutes each batch

# smoked mussel fritters

2 x 3½-oz cans smoked
   mussels, drained
1 cup all-purpose flour
1 teaspoon baking powder
1 teaspoon salt
1 small red bell pepper,
   seeded and finely diced
2 tablespoons chopped
   cilantro
½ teaspoon cayenne pepper
1 egg, lightly beaten
4½ tablespoons beer
1 tablespoon lime juice
vegetable oil, for deep-frying
lime wedges, to serve

**Sauce:**
¼ cup Mayonnaise (see page
   125)
1 teaspoon wholegrain
   mustard
juice ½ lime
½ teaspoon clear honey

- Roughly chop the mussels and place in a bowl with the flour, baking powder, salt, red pepper, cilantro, and cayenne, and stir well.
- Beat in the egg, beer, and lime juice to form a soft dropping batter.
- Heat 2 inches vegetable oil in a deep, heavy-based saucepan until it reaches 350–375°F, or until a cube of bread browns in 30 seconds.
- Drop teaspoons of the mussel batter into the hot oil in batches, and fry for about 3 minutes, until golden. Drain on paper towels and keep warm in a moderate oven while cooking the rest.
- Combine all the sauce ingredients in a bowl. Serve the fritters with the sauce and some lime wedges to squeeze.

There is a wide selection of interesting snack and appetizer recipes here, although recipes such as Mini Chicken Kiev, Smoked Salmon and Poached Egg Salad on Muffins, and Piedmontese Peppers can all provide simple but satisfying light lunch or supper dishes.

# bigger
# bites

8 zucchini flowers
8 anchovy fillets

**Batter:**
1 egg, separated
1 tablespoon olive oil
7 tablespons light beer
9 tablespoons all-purpose flour
1 tablespoon chopped fresh basil
salt and pepper
vegetable oil, for deep-frying

Serves: 4–8
**Preparation time:** 10 minutes, plus resting time
**Cooking time:** 6–8 minutes

# anchovy-stuffed zucchini flowers

*Even if you do not have a garden, zucchini can be grown in pots on a windowsill very successfully. Some specialist greengrocers can supply the flowers in season.*

- First, make the batter. In a large bowl beat the egg yolk, oil, beer, flour, and basil to make a smooth batter. Season with salt and pepper, cover, and set aside for 30 minutes.
- Carefully clean the zucchini flowers. Wash and dry the anchovies and slip an anchovy fillet into each flower.
- Heat 2 inches vegetable oil in a deep saucepan until it reaches 350–375°F, or until a cube of bread browns in 30 seconds.
- Dip the stuffed flowers into the batter 2 at a time. Deep-fry in the hot oil for 1–1½ minutes, until crisp and golden. Drain on paper towels and keep warm in a moderate oven while frying the rest. Serve hot.

Serves: 12
**Preparation time:** 20 minutes
**Cooking time:** 15 minutes

# *garbanzo-bean and chard* tortilla

*This is a delicious and slightly unusual variation of the more classic potato tortilla. The garbanzo beans add a lovely nutty flavor to the omelet.*

6 tablespoons extra-virgin
   olive oil
1 onion, chopped
4 garlic cloves, crushed
½ teaspoon crushed chile
   flakes
1 lb chard leaves
1 × 14-oz can garbanzo beans,
   drained
6 eggs, beaten
2 tablespoons chopped fresh
   parsley
salt and pepper

- Heat 4 tablespoons of the oil in a large non-stick, heavy-based skillet. Add the onion, garlic, and chile flakes, and fry gently for 10 minutes, until softened and lightly golden.
- Meanwhile, wash and dry the chard, and cut away and discard the thick central white stalk. Shred the leaves. Stir the chard into the onion mixture with the garbanzo beans and cook gently for 5 minutes.
- Beat the eggs in a bowl, add the parsley, and season with salt and pepper. Stir in the garbanzo-bean mixture.
- Wipe out the pan, then add the remaining oil. Pour in the egg and garbanzo-bean mixture, and cook over a low heat for 10 minutes, until the tortilla is almost cooked through.
- Carefully slide the tortilla out onto a large plate, invert the skillet over the tortilla and then flip it back into the skillet.
- Return the skillet to the heat and continue to cook for a further 5 minutes, until cooked through. Allow to cool to room temperature and serve cut into squares.

Serves: 4 as an appetizer
**Preparation time:** 10 minutes
**Cooking time:** 40–45 minutes, plus cooling time

# roasted new potatoes

## *with smoked salmon and caviar filling*

16 small new potatoes

2 tablespoons olive oil

1 tablespoon chopped fresh rosemary

1 tablespoon chopped fresh sage

sea salt, for sprinkling

½ cup crème fraîche

4 oz smoked salmon, cut into strips

3 teaspoons lumpfish caviar

1 tablespoon snipped fresh chives

pepper

lemon wedges, to serve, optional

*A delicious combination, well worth the time spent assembling.*

○ Preheat the oven to 400°F. Place the potatoes in a roasting pan, add the olive oil, herbs, and some sea salt, and toss well. Put the roasting pan on the top shelf of the oven, and roast for 40–45 minutes, stirring occasionally, until the potatoes are crisp on the outside and very soft in the center.

○ Remove the potatoes from the oven and leave to cool for 5 minutes. Cut a cross in the top of each potato and press open slightly. Transfer them to a plate and top each with a spoonful of crème fraîche, salmon, caviar, and chives. Serve the potatoes at once with plenty of freshly ground black pepper and lemon wedges, if wished.

Serves: 12
**Preparation time:** 10 minutes
**Cooking time:** 30 minutes, plus resting time

# Spanish tortilla

⅔ cup extra-virgin olive oil
1½ lb potatoes, thinly sliced
1 large onion, sliced
5 large eggs, beaten
salt and pepper

*This is an authentic Spanish tortilla, which is traditionally made with just eggs, potatoes, onions, and seasoning, and cooked in a large amount of olive oil.*

- Heat all but 2 tablespoons of the oil in an 8-inch non-stick skillet. Add the potato slices and onions, and cook for 15 minutes, stirring frequently, until the potatoes and onion are golden and tender.
- Stir the potato mixture into the beaten eggs and season generously with salt and pepper. Set aside for 15 minutes. Clean out the skillet.
- Heat the remaining oil in the clean skillet, then tip in the tortilla mixture. Cook over a low heat for 10 minutes, until almost cooked through. Carefully slide the tortilla onto a large plate, invert the skillet over the tortilla, then flip the tortilla back into the skillet
- Return the skillet to the heat and cook for a further 5 minutes or until the tortilla is cooked on both sides. Allow to cool and serve the tortilla at room temperature cut into wedges.

2 large heads garlic
⅔ cup extra-virgin olive oil
2 sprigs fresh rosemary, bruised
salt and pepper

**To Serve:**
wedge ripe Brie
crusty bread

Serves: 4
**Preparation time:** 5 minutes
**Cooking time:** 1¼ hours

# baked garlic
## *with Brie*

*This classic Californian appetizer can be accompanied by a wedge of Camembert, instead of the Brie. Make sure the cheese is nice and ripe for the best results.*

- Preheat the oven to 400°F. Cut a small slice from the top of each head of garlic and sit them in a small baking pan. Pour over half the oil, top with the rosemary sprigs, and season well with salt and pepper. Cover with foil and bake for 1 hour. Remove the foil, baste, and bake for a further 15–20 minutes, until caramelized.
- Split each garlic head in two and transfer each half to a small plate. Drizzle over the remaining oil and serve with a wedge of Brie and plenty of crusty bread.

3 large sole, cut into quarter
  fillets, skinned, washed, and
  dried
¼ cup Anchovy Butter (see
  page 106), softened
12 sun-dried tomatoes in oil,
  drained
4 oz mozzarella cheese, cut
  into 12 dice
olive oil, for greasing
green salad, to serve


Serves: 4
**Preparation time:** 10 minutes
**Cooking time:** 8 – 10 minutes

# rolled skewered sole fillets
## *with tomatoes and mozzarella*

*Here quarter fillets of sole are spread with anchovy butter and rolled up with a sun-dried tomato and a cube of mozzarella. These are then threaded onto skewers and broiled until the fish is cooked and the cheese has melted. You will need 4 skewers.*

- Spread the underside of each fish fillet with a little anchovy butter. Place 1 sun-dried tomato and a cube of mozzarella at the narrow end of each fillet. Roll up tightly to enclose the filling and thread 3 rolled fillets onto each skewer. Spread the remaining anchovy butter all over the rolled fish.
- Preheat the broiler. Place the skewers on a broiler pan, lined with foil and greased, and cook for 8–10 minutes, turning frequently, until the fish is cooked and the cheese in the middle has melted. Serve at once with a crisp green salad.

# Thai-style crab cakes *with dipping sauce*

- In a bowl beat the flour, baking powder, and egg with the fish sauce, lime juice, and chile sauce until smooth. Stir in the crabmeat, lime leaves, and herbs, and season with a little salt and pepper. Set aside for 30 minutes to infuse the flavors.
- Meanwhile, prepare the sauce. Put the vinegar, sugar, chile flakes, and salt in a small saucepan and heat gently until the sugar dissolves. Bring to a boil and then remove from the heat to cool.
- Heat a shallow layer of oil in a heavy-based skillet. Whisk 2 tablespoons of cold water into the crab mixture and drop heaping teaspoons of it into the oil. Fry for 1 minute on each side, until golden.
- Drain on paper towels and keep warm in a hot oven while frying the remaining cakes. Serve hot with the dipping sauce.

Serves: 4–8
**Preparation time:** 25 minutes, plus infusing time
**Cooking time:** 2 minutes each batch

9 tablespoons all-purpose flour
½ teaspoon baking powder
1 egg, beaten
1 tablespoon Thai fish sauce, (nam pla)
1 tablespoon lime juice
1½ teaspoons chile sauce
⅔ cup crabmeat
4 lime leaves, finely shredded
1 tablespoon chopped fresh cilantro
½ tablespoon chopped fresh mint
½ tablespoon chopped fresh basil
salt and pepper
vegetable oil, for shallow-frying

**Dipping Sauce:**
¼ cup rice vinegar
7 teaspoons superfine sugar
¼ teaspoon crushed chile flakes
½ teaspoon salt

1 lb fresh spinach

⅔ cup extra-virgin olive oil

1 onion, finely chopped

4 scallions chopped

1 garlic cloves, crushed

1 teaspoons dried oregano

2 tablespoons chopped fresh parsley

1 tablespoon chopped fresh dill

2 tablespoons chopped fresh mint

½ cup ricotta cheese

½ cup freshly grated Parmesan cheese

1 egg, lightly beaten

12 sheets frozen phyllo pastry, thawed

salt and pepper

Serves: 8
**Preparation time:** 45 minutes
**Cooking time:** 35–40 minutes, plus cooling time

# spanakopita

- Wash the spinach leaves and place them in a large saucepan with just the water clinging to the leaves. Stir over a medium heat for 2–3 minutes until the spinach is wilted. Drain well and squeeze out all the excess liquid. Chop finely.
- Heat ¼ cup of the oil in a skillet, and fry the onion, scallions, garlic, and oregano for 10 minutes, until softened. Stir in the chopped spinach and fresh herbs, and remove from the heat.
- Transfer the mixture to a bowl and stir in the ricotta, Parmesan, and egg. Season with salt and pepper and mix until evenly combined.
- Preheat the oven to 375°F. Take 1 sheet of phyllo pastry and brush with oil, then place in an oiled 8 x 10-inch baking pan. Repeat with a further 5 sheets of pastry. Spread the filling over the pastry and top with the remaining sheets of pastry, brushing with oil as you go.
- Using a sharp knife, score the top of the pie with a diamond pattern, cutting down as far as the filling. Brush over any remaining oil and bake for 35–40 minutes, until the pastry is golden. Allow to cool for 10 minutes, then cut into squares and serve warm.

Serves: 4
**Preparation time:** 20 minutes, plus soaking time
**Cooking time:** 25–30 minutes

# *bulgur stuffed*
# tomatoes

⅓ cup bulgur wheat

4 beefsteak tomatoes

2 tablespoons olive oil, plus
extra for drizzling

1 onion, finely chopped

2 tablespoons pine nuts

2 garlic cloves, crushed

1 teaspoon ground cumin

2 tablespoons raisins

2 tablespoons chopped fresh
parsley

1 tablespoon chopped fresh
mint

1 cup grated Cheddar cheese

salt and pepper

◉ Soak the bulgur in plenty of hot water for 30 minutes, drain well, and squeeze out the excess liquid.

◉ Cut a thin slice from the top of each tomato, discard the seeds, then scoop out and finely chop the flesh.

◉ Heat the oil in a skillet and fry the onion, pine nuts, crushed garlic, and cumin for 10 minutes until softened. Stir in the bulgur and the tomato pulp, and fry for a further 5 minutes.

◉ Remove the skillet from the heat and stir in the raisins, parsley, mint, and half the cheese, and season to taste with salt and pepper. Spoon the mixture into the empty tomato shells and scatter over the remaining cheese.

◉ Preheat the oven to 375°F. Transfer the tomatoes to a small baking dish, drizzle over a little extra oil, and bake for 25–30 minutes, until the tomatoes are very soft and the cheese crisp and golden.

# spare ribs

*Cooking the ribs in water and vinegar tenderizes the meat so that when baked, the meat literally melts in the mouth.*

1 lb pork spare ribs

1 tablespoon distilled malt
vinegar

1 tablespoon sesame oil

¼ cup white wine vinegar

2 tablespoons dark soy sauce

1 tablespoon ketchup

1 garlic clove, crushed

1 teaspoon grated fresh ginger

2 tablespoons clear honey

¼ teaspoon Chinese five spice
powder

pinch of chile powder

◉ Place the spare ribs in a saucepan, and add the malt vinegar and enough water to cover. Bring to a boil, skimming the surface, and simmer for 20 minutes.

◉ Drain the ribs and transfer to a roasting pan. Preheat the oven to 425°F. Meanwhile, place all the remaining ingredients in a small pan with ¼ cup water and bring to a boil. Pour over the ribs and toss well to coat.

◉ Cover the roasting pan with foil and bake for 30 minutes. Remove the foil, and baste the ribs by stirring once. Return to the oven and cook for a further 30 minutes, basting occasionally, until tender. Cool slightly and serve with a finger bowl.

Serves: 4
**Preparation time:** 25 minutes
**Cooking time:** 1 hour

1 tablespoon groundnut oil

½ cup ground pork

½ teaspoon crushed chile flakes

½ tablespoon dark soy sauce

½ tablespoon soft dark brown sugar

½ tablespoon dry sherry

1 tablespoon white wine vinegar

⅔ cup chopped creamed coconut

⅔ cup beansprouts

2 tablespoons chopped fresh cilantro

6 large Belgian endive leaves

salt and pepper

cilantro sprigs, to garnish

Serves: 6
**Preparation time:** 5 minutes
**Cooking time:** 15–20 minutes

# sweet and sour ground pork

- Heat the oil in a skillet and stir-fry the pork and chile flakes for 5 minutes, until the pork is browned. Add the soy sauce, sugar, and sherry, and stir-fry for a further 1 minute.
- Stir in the vinegar, coconut, and 2–3 tablespoons water until blended and then simmer gently for 10 minutes. Remove from the heat and stir in the beansprouts and cilantro, then season to taste with salt and pepper.
- Pile the pork mixture into the endive leaves, garnish with cilantro sprigs, and serve immediately.

Serves: 4
**Preparation time:** 10 minutes, plus marinating time
**Cooking time:** 6–8 minutes

## *spicy broiled*
# lamb cutlets

8 small lamb cutlets

2 teaspoons paprika

¼ teaspoon cayenne pepper

1 tablespoon sesame seeds

1 tablespoon chopped fresh
  thyme

2 tablespoons olive oil

1 tablespoon lemon juice

salt and pepper

**Mint and Garlic Sauce:**

½ cup yogurt

1 garlic clove, crushed

2 tablespoons chopped fresh
  mint

pinch of sugar

- Trim the cutlets of excess fat and place in a shallow dish. Place the paprika, cayenne, sesame seeds, and thyme in a spice grinder or use a pestle and mortar and blend to a powder. Transfer to a dish and stir in the oil, lemon juice, and a little salt and pepper.
- Pour over the lamb and rub well into the meat. Cover and marinate for several hours or overnight. Remove from the refrigerator at least 1 hour before cooking.
- Prepare the sauce. In a bowl combine all the ingredients, season with salt and pepper to taste, and set aside until required.
- Preheat the broiler. Place the marinated cutlets on a rack set over the broiler pan and broil for 3–4 minutes on each side, until golden and cooked through.
- Allow the cutlets to cool slightly and serve with the Mint and Garlic Sauce to dip.

## *spiced* lamb kebabs

1 lb ground lamb

1 tablespoon lemon juice

1 small onion, minced

2 garlic cloves, crushed

1 teaspoon grated fresh ginger

2 tablespoons chopped fresh
  parsley

1 tablespoon chopped fresh
  mint

2 teaspoons ground coriander

1 teaspoon ground turmeric

1 teaspoon ground cumin

1 teaspoon ground cinnamon

1 tablespoon chile sauce

1 egg, beaten

salt and pepper

yogurt or Aïoli (see page 125),
  to serve

*Soaking the bamboo skewers in cold water for 30 minutes before use stops them from burning in the broiler.*

- Combine all the ingredients except the egg in a large bowl until evenly blended. Season with salt and pepper. Cover and leave to infuse for at least 1 hour.
- Soak 16 bamboo skewers in cold water for 30 minutes and pat dry. Stir the egg into the lamb and mix well. Divide the meat mixture into 16 and shape into small sausages.
- Thread 1 sausage shape onto each skewer. Cook over a barbecue or on a wire rack in a preheated broiler for 10 minutes, turning from time to time, until browned and cooked through. Cool slightly and serve the lamb kebabs with yogurt or Aïoli.

Serves: 8
**Preparation time:** 10 minutes, plus marinating time
**Cooking time**: 10 minutes

Serves: 8
**Preparation time:** 40 minutes
**Cooking time:** 15–20 minutes

# salmon and potato parcels

8 oz potatoes, peeled

1 tablespoon butter

½ onion, finely chopped

¼ teaspoon fennel seeds, roughly ground

1 teaspoon finely grated lemon zest

1 tablespoon chopped fresh dill

6 oz smoked salmon, finely chopped

1 tablespoon lemon juice

1 egg yolk

1 × 17¼ oz package frozen puff pastry, thawed

salt and pepper

**Egg Glaze:**

1 small egg

1 tablespoon milk

- Cook the potatoes in lightly salted boiling water for about 15 minutes, until done. Drain well and mash with a fork (the texture of the potato mash should remain fairly rough).

- Melt the butter in a small saucepan and fry the onion, fennel, and lemon zest for 10 minutes, until very soft. Transfer to a bowl and stir in the mashed potato, dill, salmon, lemon juice, and egg yolk until well blended, and season with salt and pepper.

- Roll out the pastry to form a thin rectangle 7 x 14 inches and cut into 6 squares measuring 3½ inches. Divide the filling between the squares, placing a mound slightly off center. Dampen the edges of the pastry and fold each square in half diagonally to form a triangle. Press together to seal.

- Preheat the oven to 425°F. Transfer the triangles to a lightly greased baking sheet. Beat the ingredients for the egg glaze together and season with a pinch of salt. Brush the glaze lightly over the pastry. Bake for 15–20 minutes, until puffed up and golden. Serve hot.

Makes: 14
**Preparation time:** 45 minutes, plus rising and soaking time
**Cooking time:** 15–20 minutes, plus cooling time

# piroshki

*Piroshki (or pirozhki) is the Russian name given to these small stuffed bread parcels. The stuffing can be made using meat or fish as well as a vegetable mixture.*

**Dough:**

2 cups all-purpose flour

½ teaspoon salt

2 teaspoons fast-acting dry yeast

1 teaspoon sugar

3–5 tablespoons warm milk

1 small egg, beaten

2 tablespoons butter, melted

**Filling:**

½ cup dried ceps

2 tablespoons butter

4 large scallions, finely chopped

2 garlic cloves, crushed

1 cup finely chopped chestnut mushrooms

2 tablespoons chopped fresh dill

2 oz cooked rice

2 hard boiled eggs, finely chopped

2 tablespoons sour cream

salt and pepper

1 recipe Egg Glaze (see page 73)

○ Start by making the dough. Sift the flour and salt into the bowl of a food mixer and stir in the yeast and sugar. With the dough hook on a low setting, gradually blend in the milk, egg, and melted butter to form a soft, slightly sticky dough. Knead for 10 minutes.

○ If you wish to make the dough by hand, sift the flour and salt into a bowl and stir in the yeast. Make a well in the center and gradually work in the milk, egg, and butter to form a soft, slightly sticky dough. Turn out and knead on a lightly floured surface for 10 minutes until the dough is smooth and elastic.

○ Cover the bowl with plastic wrap and leave to rise in a warm place until doubled in size, about 1½–2 hours.

○ Put the dried ceps into a bowl, add ⅔ cup boiling water and set aside to soak for 30 minutes. Drain and reserve the liquid, chop and reserve the ceps.

○ Melt the butter in a skillet and fry the scallions and garlic for 5 minutes. Add the ceps and chestnut mushrooms and continue to fry over a high heat for 5–6 minutes, until the mushrooms are golden.

○ Add the reserved cep liquid and boil until it has almost evaporated. Transfer to a bowl and stir in the remaining ingredients, except the egg glaze. Season with salt and pepper to taste. Set aside to cool.

○ Punch down the dough and then divide into 14 balls. Roll each one out on a lightly floured surface to a 4-inch round.

○ Take spoonfuls of the mushroom filling and place in the center of each round. Brush the edges with a little egg glaze, pull up the sides, and pinch together across the center to seal in the filling.

○ Transfer the piroshki to lightly greased baking sheets, cover loosely with greased plastic wrap, and leave to rise for 20–30 minutes. Preheat the oven to 425°F.

○ Bake for 15–20 minutes, until risen and golden. Allow to cool for about 10 minutes. Serve warm.

# smoked salmon and poached egg salad *on muffins*

1 tablespoon distilled white
  vinegar
4 eggs
2 plain muffins, halved
⅓ recipe Anchovy Butter (see
  page 106)
6 cups chopped frisée lettuce
8 oz smoked salmon
1 tablespoon poppy seeds
snipped fresh chives,
  to garnish

**Dressing:**
2 teaspoons champagne or
  white wine vinegar
1 teaspoon Dijon mustard
1 tablespoon snipped fresh
  chives
6 tablespoons extra-virgin
  olive oil
2 ripe tomatoes, peeled,
  seeded, and diced
salt and pepper

*For hard poached eggs, follow the instructions below but cook the eggs in the water for 3–4 minutes.*

- First poach the eggs. Bring a small skillet of water to a gentle simmer, add the vinegar, and then carefully break in the eggs to fit closely together. Remove the skillet from the heat and leave the eggs in the water to poach until just set.
- Meanwhile, preheat the broiler and toast both sides of the muffins until golden, then split, spread the insides with anchovy butter, and return to the broiler for a further 1–2 minutes, until golden.
- Blend all the dressing ingredients except the tomatoes. Taste and adjust the seasoning, if necessary, and toss half with the frisée lettuce. Stir the diced tomato into the remaining dressing.
- Arrange the muffins on serving plates, top each with some of the smoked salmon and the dressed frisée, and sprinkle over the poppy seeds. Carefully remove the poached eggs from the water with a slotted spoon, drain on paper towels, and place 1 egg on top of each muffin. Pour the tomato dressing around each muffin and serve at once, garnished with the snipped chives.

Serves: 4
**Preparation time:** 20 minutes
**Cooking time:** 10 minutes

**Clockwise from far left:** Seafood Escabèche; Potato Bravas; Butterfly Chile Shrimp; and Fava Beans with Serrano Ham

# little dishes

Why not prepare around six of the dishes in the following chapter and arrange them in pretty colored bowls in the center of your dinner table? Supply large plates and plenty of napkins and get your guests to help themselves.

Serves: 4–6
**Preparation time:** 20–25 minutes, plus marinating time
**Cooking time:** 3 minutes

# *butterfly* chile shrimp

12 large raw shrimp,
  about 1 lb
¼ cup extra-virgin olive oil,
  plus extra to serve
4 garlic cloves, sliced
½ teaspoon crushed chile
  flakes
grated zest and juice 1 lemon
salt and pepper
¼ cup chopped fresh parsley,
  to garnish

**To Serve:**
lemon wedges
fresh bread

- Using a sharp serrated knife, cut down the back of the shrimp through the shell, but do not cut completely in half. Pull out and discard the black vein and wash and dry the shrimp. Butterfly the shrimp out by turning them flesh side down and pressing flat.
- Combine the olive oil, garlic, chile flakes, and lemon zest and juice, and season with a little salt and pepper. Place the shrimp on a large tray, pour over the oil mixture, cover, and chill for 2 hours.
- Heat a large iron griddle or heavy-based skillet. Place the shrimp, shell side down, on the hot skillet in a single layer and cook for 1–2 minutes, until the shells shrivel and the flesh starts to turn pink. Flip the shrimp and cook for a further 30 seconds.
- Transfer the shrimp to a serving dish, garnish with the parsley, and drizzle over some more olive oil. Serve with lemon wedges and fresh bread.

# fava beans
## *with Serrano ham*

1 tablespoon olive oil
4 oz piece Serrano ham, diced
2 garlic cloves, sliced
2½ cups freshly podded fava
  beans – 1½ lb in the pod
5 tablespoons dry white wine
2 tomatoes, peeled, seeded,
  and diced
1 tablespoon chopped
  fresh dill
salt and pepper

*Serrano ham is a Spanish cured ham similar to the Italian prosciutto, which can be substituted. You will need to ask for the ham to be cut into one thick slice for this dish.*

- Heat the oil in a skillet, add the ham, and fry briefly to brown on all sides. Lower the heat, add the garlic and beans, and fry gently for 5 minutes.
- Add the wine and tomatoes, bring to a boil, cover, and simmer for 10–15 minutes, until the beans are tender. Season to taste with salt and pepper, stir in the dill, and serve at once.

Serves: 4
**Preparation time:** 12 minutes
**Cooking time:** 15–20 minutes

Serves: 4
**Preparation time:** 25–30 minutes, plus chilling and resting time
**Cooking time:** 15 minutes

# *seafood* **escabèche**

16 large mussels, scrubbed
8 oz baby squid, cleaned
8 oz peeled small raw shrimp,
   deveined (see page 78)
2 garlic cloves, chopped
1 small red chile, seeded and
   chopped
¼ cup dry sherry
1 tablespoon chopped basil,
   to garnish
bread, to serve

**Marinade:**
⅔ cup extra-virgin olive oil
2 shallots, chopped
3 tablespoons white wine
   vinegar
pinch of sugar
1 tablespoon drained and
   chopped capers in brine
salt and pepper

*Escabèche means "marinated" and is a classic Spanish tapas dish. Other fish, and even vegetables, can be used as well as seafood.*

- Prepare the seafood. Remove any beards still attached to the mussels. Cut the squid into rings and the tentacles in half, if large, and wash well. Wash and dry the shrimp.
- Put the mussels into a saucepan with the garlic, chile, and sherry, cover, and steam for 4–5 minutes, until all the mussels are opened (discard any that remain closed). Remove the mussels with a slotted spoon and set aside.
- Poach the shrimp in the mussel liquid for 4–5 minutes, until cooked. Poach the squid for 2–3 minutes, until cooked. Remove with a slotted spoon and add to the mussels. Reserve 2 tablespoons of the cooking liquid and leave to cool.
- Combine all the marinade ingredients and stir in the reserved poaching liquid. Pour over the cold seafood, toss well, and chill for several hours.
- Return the escabèche to room temperature for 1 hour, scatter over the basil, and serve with bread.

# **potato bravas**

2 lb small potatoes
2 tablespoons olive oil
sea salt

**Sauce:**
¼ cup olive oil
1 tablespoon tomato paste
1 tablespoon red wine vinegar
1 teaspoon chile sauce
2 teaspoons paprika pepper
salt and pepper

- Cut the potatoes into ½-inch-thick slices and place in a single layer on a baking sheet. Preheat the oven to 450°F.
- Brush the potatoes with olive oil, sprinkle with sea salt, and bake for 20 minutes. Turn the potatoes over and bake for a further 10 minutes, until crisp and golden.
- Combine the sauce ingredients with 2 tablespoons water in a sauté pan. Add the cooked potatoes and heat through. Season to taste with salt and pepper, and serve hot.

Serves: 4
**Preparation time:** 5 minutes
**Cooking time:** 30 minutes

Serves: 4
**Preparation time:** 10 minutes, plus marinating time
**Cooking time:** 5 minutes

# chile scallops

8 large scallops in their shells
2 tablespoons sunflower oil,
  plus extra for frying
1 teaspoon sesame oil
1 tablespoon dark soy sauce
1 teaspoon grated root ginger
pinch of Chinese five spice
  powder
1 tablespoon Thai red curry
  paste
1 tablespoon chopped fresh
  cilantro
1–2 tablespoons sesame
  seeds
⅔ cup fish or vegetable stock

**To Garnish:**
cilantro sprigs
2 red chiles, sliced

*You can use shelled scallops for this dish, and serve them in small dishes rather than in their shells.*

- Carefully remove the scallops from their shells by snipping through the muscle that attaches them (or ask your fishmonger to clean the scallops for you). Wash and reserve the deep shells. Wash and dry the scallops, discarding the muscle.
- Combine the remaining ingredients, except the sesame seeds and stock, in a shallow dish. Add the scallops, toss well to coat, and leave to marinate for at least 1 hour.
- Remove the scallops from their marinade and coat with the sesame seeds. Scrape the marinade into a saucepan and add the stock. Simmer until reduced by half.
- Heat a little oil on a griddle or in a heavy-based skillet. When very hot, add the scallops and fry for 1 minute on each side. Serve the scallops either in their shells or in small dishes. Pour the marinade over the scallops and garnish with cilantro and chiles.

Serves: 4–6
**Preparation time:** 20 minutes, plus overnight soaking
**Cooking time:** 15 minutes

# *brandade of*
# **salt cod**

6 oz salt cod

⅔ cup olive oil

⅔ cup whole milk (or milk and cream mixed)

2 large garlic cloves, crushed

2 tablespoons chopped fresh chives

1 teaspoon lemon juice

pepper

**To Serve:**

vegetable crudités

French bread

*Salt cod is available from good fishmongers or specialist food shops. It needs to be soaked in several changes of cold water for 24 hours before cooking.*

○ Place the salt cod in a large bowl and cover with cold water. Leave to soak for 24 hours, changing the water several times if possible.

○ Drain the cod, rinse well, and place in a saucepan. Add enough cold water to cover, bring to a boil, and poach gently for 10 minutes. Drain, cool, and dry well. Discard the bones and skin, and flake the flesh.

○ Place the oil, milk, and garlic in a saucepan and heat gently until the mixture just begins to boil.

○ Put the fish into a blender or food processor and pulse briefly. Then, with the blade running, gradually pour in the oil mixture through the funnel until a smooth creamy paste is made.

○ Transfer the brandade to a bowl, stir in the chives, add the lemon juice, and season with black pepper. Serve the brandade with a selection of fresh vegetable crudités and some French bread.

Serves: 4
**Preparation time:** 10 minutes, plus marinating time

# *Moroccan*
# carrot salad

1 lb carrots
1 garlic clove, crushed
1 teaspoon salt
pinch of sugar
6 tablespoons extra-virgin
  olive oil
2 tablespoons red wine
  vinegar
½ teaspoon ground cumin
¼ teaspoon cayenne pepper
1 tablespoon chopped fresh
  cilantro
pepper

○ Using the grater attachment of a food processor (or the finest side of a box grater) thinly grate the carrots. Transfer to a strainer and drain any excess liquid.

○ Combine all the remaining ingredients, adjusting the seasoning to taste. Stir into the grated carrot, cover, and leave to marinate in the refrigerator for at least 1 hour. Serve slightly chilled.

# cauliflower with anchovy and garlic sauce

1 large head cauliflower,
  trimmed
½ x 2-oz can anchovy fillets,
  drained
½ recipe Aïoli (see page 125)
pepper
1 tablespoon chopped fresh
  parsley, to garnish

○ Cut the cauliflower into large florets and steam for 10–12 minutes, until tender. Transfer to a large shallow dish with 1 tablespoon of the cooking liquid.

○ Finely chop the anchovy fillets and stir into the Aïoli. Pour the Aïoli over the cauliflower florets while still warm and toss to coat. Season with a little black pepper and garnish with chopped parsley. Serve warm.

Serves: 8
**Preparation time:** 5–6 minutes
**Cooking time:** 10–12 minutes

Serves: 6
**Preparation time:** 5 minutes, plus overnight soaking
**Cooking time:** 2 hours

# large lima beans
## *in tomato sauce*

1½ cups dried lima beans, soaked overnight in cold water

2 × 14 oz-cans chopped tomatoes

1⅓ cups vegetable stock

2 garlic cloves, chopped

2 tablespoons extra-virgin olive oil

1 tablespoon chopped fresh oregano

2 bay leaves

1 teaspoon superfine sugar

1 tablespoon lemon juice

2 tablespoons chopped fresh dill

salt and pepper

crusty bread, to serve

*This is a classic Greek dish known as* Gigantes Plaki *and can be found in tavernas throughout Greece, where it is served as part of a* meze.

○ Drain the soaked beans, wash well, and set aside. Put the tomatoes, stock, garlic, olive oil, oregano, bay leaves, and sugar in a large saucepan and bring to a boil. Stir in the beans, return to a boil, cover, and simmer over a low heat for 1½ hours or until the beans are very tender. Remove the lid and simmer for a further 30 minutes, until the sauce is reduced and thickened.

○ Stir in the lemon juice and chopped dill, season with salt and pepper, and leave to cool slightly. Serve warm with some crusty bread.

Serves: 4
**Preparation time:** 10 minutes
**Cooking time:** 4–6 minutes each batch

# *broiled*
# Mediterranean vegetables

1 small eggplant
1 large zucchini
1 red bell pepper, seeded
1 red onion
3 garlic cloves
1 teaspoon cumin seeds
1 tablespoon chopped fresh
 thyme
1 tablespoon balsamic vinegar
⅔ cup extra-virgin olive oil
salt and pepper
1 tablespoon chopped fresh
 basil

○ First prepare the vegetables. Cut the eggplant into 8 slices, the zucchini into ¼-inch-thick diagonal slices, the pepper into thick strips, and the onion into thick wedges. Place in a large bowl.

○ In a spice grinder or using a pestle and mortar, mash the garlic, cumin seeds, and thyme to a paste. Stir in the balsamic vinegar and ¼ cup of the oil, and season with salt and pepper. Pour over the vegetables and toss well to coat.

○ Preheat the broiler, then broil the vegetables a few at a time for 2–3 minutes on each side, until charred and tender.

○ Transfer the vegetables to a warmed serving plate, drizzle over the remaining olive oil, and scatter over the basil. Serve warm.

2 large herrings, filleted

juice 2 lemons

½ cup crème fraîche

1 tablespoon hot horseradish sauce

salt and pepper

1 tablespoon chopped fresh dill, to garnish

**Marinade:**

⅔ cup white wine vinegar

½ cup superfine sugar

1 garlic clove, sliced

1 small red onion, sliced

2 bay leaves

2 sprigs fresh dill, bruised

1 teaspoon all spice berries, bruised

6 white peppercorns

Serves: 4

**Preparation time:** 25 minutes, plus marinating and resting time

# marinated herring
## *with horseradish cream*

- Using a pair of tweezers, pull out as many of the tiny bones from the herring fillets as possible. Wash and dry well. Place the fillets skin side down in a ceramic dish and pour over the lemon juice. Cover and chill for 2 hours.
- Meanwhile, prepare the marinade. Combine all the ingredients in a bowl with ⅔ cup cold water and set aside. Stir occasionally to dissolve the sugar.
- Drain the herrings and discard the juices. Cut the fish into bite-sized pieces, return to the dish, and pour over the marinade. Cover and leave to marinate overnight in the refrigerator.
- Remove the herring fillets from the marinade and allow them to return to room temperature for 1 hour. Discard the marinade.
- Combine the crème fraîche and horseradish sauce in a small bowl and season with a little salt and pepper to taste.
- Arrange the herrings on a platter with the bowl of horseradish cream and garnish with chopped fresh dill.

Serves: 8
**Preparation time:** 10 minutes
**Cooking time:** 8–10 minutes,

# *pasta with*
# herb sauce

8 oz dried pasta

7 tablespoons extra-virgin
olive oil, plus extra to serve

grated zest and juice 1 small
lemon

1 garlic clove, crushed

⅔ cup fresh herbs; to include
basil, chervil, chives, dill and
parsley

4 anchovy fillets in oil, drained
and chopped

1 tablespoon chopped capers
in brine, drained

salt and pepper

○ Bring a large pan of lightly salted water to a rolling boil, add the pasta, return to a boil, and cook for 8–10 minutes, until *al dente*.

○ Meanwhile, place all the remaining ingredients in a blender or food processor and blend to form a smooth sauce. Season to taste with salt and pepper.

○ Strain the pasta, reserving 2 tablespoons of the cooking water. Toss the pasta with the herb sauce, adding the reserved cooking liquid. Leave to cool to room temperature. Taste and adjust the seasoning, adding a little extra olive oil if needed.

Serves: 4
**Preparation time:** 15 minutes
**Cooking time:** 10 minutes

# kidneys cooked with sherry

8 veal or lamb kidneys

juice 1 lemon

2 tablespoons olive oil

1 garlic clove, crushed

⅔ cup chopped pancetta

¼ cup dry sherry

2 tablespoons chopped fresh
  parsley

salt and pepper

○ Halve the kidneys and cut out the white cores. Place the kidneys in a bowl, add the lemon juice, and set aside for 10 minutes.

○ Heat the oil in a skillet. When hot, add the kidneys, garlic and pancetta and stir over a high heat for 3–4 minutes, until browned.

○ Add the sherry and simmer for a further 3–4 minutes, until the sherry is reduced and the kidneys cooked through. Sprinkle over the parsley, season to taste with salt and pepper, and serve at once.

Serves: 4
**Preparation time:** 5 minutes
**Cooking time:** 15–20 minutes

# roasted vine tomatoes
## *with goat cheese*

1 lb cherry tomatoes on the vine

2 garlic cloves, sliced

2 sprigs fresh thyme

6 tablespoons extra-virgin olive oil

6 oz fresh goat cheese

salt and pepper

toast, to serve

- Preheat the oven to 450°F. Place the tomatoes still attached to the vine in a shallow roasting pan. Scatter over the garlic and thyme, and drizzle over the oil.
- Place in the oven for 15–20 minutes, until browned and softened. Spoon the tomatoes onto toasted bread, top with the goat cheese, and pour over the pan juices. Serve immediately.

Serves: 4
**Preparation time:** 25 – 30 minutes, plus overnight chilling
**Cooking time:** 20 minutes

# chicken liver pâté
## with sweet and sour onion salsa

8 oz chicken livers

1 shallot, finely chopped

¼ cup butter

3 tablespoons Madeira

3 tablespoons heavy cream

1 teaspoon pink peppercorns, crushed

salt and pepper

crisp bread or toast, to serve

**Sweet and Sour Onion Salsa:**

2 red onions, sliced

1 tablespoon olive oil

3 tablespoons balsamic vinegar

2 tablespoons soft brown sugar

1 sprig fresh rosemary, bruised

*The onion salsa with its sweet and sour flavor cuts through the rich creaminess of the pâté, making it a perfect partner. To bruise the rosemary, lightly crush it with a rolling pin; this will help to release its flavor into the salsa.*

○ Trim the chicken livers, discarding any discolored parts, then wash and dry well. Fry the shallot in the butter for 5 minutes.

○ Increase the heat and add the chicken livers. Fry for 3–4 minutes, until browned on all sides but still slightly pink in the center.

○ Remove the livers using a slotted spoon and place in a blender. Add the Madeira to the skillet and reduce by half, scraping the sediment from the base.

○ Scrape into the blender, add the cream and a little salt, and purée to a smooth paste. Pass through a fine strainer, stir in the peppercorns, and spoon into a small dish. Leave to cool and then chill overnight.

○ To make the salsa, place all the ingredients in a saucepan with ¼ cup water and season with salt and pepper. Simmer over a low heat for 20 minutes, until soft and caramelized. Leave to cool. Serve the pâté and salsa together with some crisp bread or toast.

Serves: 2– 4
**Preparation time:** 5 minutes
**Cooking time:** 15 minutes

# flageolet beans
## *with lemon, rosemary, and chile*

2 tablespoons extra-virgin
  olive oil, plus extra to serve
1 small onion, finely chopped
2 garlic cloves, chopped
1 red chile, seeded and diced
1 teaspoon chopped fresh
  rosemary
grated zest and juice ½ lemon
1 × 14-oz can flageolet beans,
  drained
1 tablespoon chopped fresh
  parsley
salt and pepper

- Heat the oil in a skillet and fry the onion, garlic, chile, rosemary, and lemon zest for 10 minutes, until softened but not browned.
- Stir in the beans, lemon juice, and 2 tablespoons of water, bring to a boil, cover, and simmer gently for 5 minutes.
- Remove from the heat, season to taste with salt and pepper, and leave to cool. Stir in the parsley and serve the beans drizzled with olive oil.

# *Pacific Rim* mussels

2 tablespoons vegetable oil
1 small onion, finely chopped
2 garlic cloves, crushed
1 teaspoon grated fresh ginger
1 teaspoon hot curry paste
¼ teaspoon ground allspice
pinch cayenne pepper
1 × 14-oz can chopped
  tomatoes
2 lime leaves, shredded
1½ lb large fresh mussels,
  scrubbed and cleaned,
  beards removed
salt and pepper
1 tablespoon chopped fresh
  cilantro, to garnish

- Heat the oil in the bottom of a double-boiler or large saucepan. Add the onion, garlic, ginger, curry paste, and spices, and fry gently for 10 minutes until softened.
- Add the chopped tomatoes and shredded lime leaves, cover, and simmer for 20 minutes, until thickened. Season to taste with salt and pepper.
- Place the mussels either in the top of the double-boiler or in a steamer set over the saucepan. Steam the mussels over the sauce for 5 minutes. Discard any mussels that do not open.
- Carefully discard one half of each mussel shell and arrange the mussels in individual serving dishes. Spoon over the sauce and serve at once, garnished with the chopped cilantro.

Serves: 6
**Preparation time:** 25 minutes
**Cooking time:** 5–10 minutes

½ cucumber, peeled, halved, and seeded

2 oz vermicelli rice noodles

1 carrot, cut into long julienne strips

1 red chile, seeded and cut into long julienne strips

2 tablespoons chopped fresh cilantro

salt

cilantro sprigs, to garnish

**Dressing:**

2 tablespoons sunflower oil

½ teaspoon sesame oil

2 teaspoons superfine sugar

2 tablespoons lime juice

1 tablespoon Thai fish sauce (nam pla)

salt and pepper

Serves: 4–6

**Preparation time:** 15 minutes, plus draining and soaking time

# *hot and sour*
# noodle and
# vegetable salad

*A fresh tasting Thai-style salad made with the clear rice noodles available in many larger supermarkets or oriental stores.*

- Sprinkle the cucumber with salt and set aside to drain for 30 minutes. Soak the noodles, covered, in boiling water for 4–6 minutes, or according to the instructions on the package. Wash and dry the cucumber; drain and dry the noodles.
- Combine all the dressing ingredients, season with salt and pepper to taste, and toss half with the noodles. Place in a large bowl.
- Cut the cucumber into long thin julienne strips and add to the noodles with the julienne strips of carrot and chile. Stir in the cilantro and the remaining dressing and serve at once, garnished with cilantro sprigs.

Summertime heralds the arrival of picnics and eating *al fresco*, and this chapter provides a whole range of exciting foods for those occasions. Wrap up the home-made Olive Foccacia with Infused Herb Oil and include some extra oil to dip the bread into, or really impress your friends with the stunning Picnic Chicken Loaf.

# breads
## and pastries

Serves: 4
**Preparation time:** 15–20 minutes, plus resting time
**Cooking time:** 10 minutes

# *shrimp and arugula*
# **piadina**

*Piadina, the precursor of the pizza, is a small disk of unleavened dough that is dry-fried on a very hot griddle.*

1 cup all-purpose flour
½ teaspoon salt
1 teaspoon butter, softened

**Topping:**
¼ cup extra-virgin olive oil,
   plus extra for serving
2 large garlic cloves, crushed
pinch of crushed chile flakes
½ teaspoon dried oregano
1 lb medium-sized fresh tiger
   shrimp, deveined
6 oz arugula
6 oz feta cheese, crumbled
pepper

- Sift the flour and salt into a bowl, make a well in the center, and work in the butter and ¼ cup tepid water to form a soft dough. Knead the dough on a lightly floured surface for 10 minutes. Wrap in plastic wrap and leave to rest for 30 minutes.

- Divide the dough into 4 pieces and roll each one out to 5-inch round. Cover with a clean dish towel while preparing the topping.

- Heat the oil in a large skillet. As soon as it stops foaming add the garlic, chile flakes, and dried oregano, stir well, and immediately add the shrimp. Fry for 3–4 minutes, until the shrimp are cooked. Stir in the arugula and cook until wilted. Keep warm.

- Heat a griddle or heavy-based skillet until hot. Cook 1 piadina dough base at a time for about 1 minute, flip over, and cook the underneath for a further 30 seconds, until dotted brown.

- Transfer the piadina to warmed plates and top with the shrimp and arugula mixture, scatter over the feta, and serve at once drizzled with extra olive oil.

1 cup ricotta cheese

1 small garlic clove, crushed

2 scallions, finely chopped

2 teaspoons lemon juice

¼ cup sun-dried tomatoes in oil, drained and finely chopped

¼ cup chopped fresh herbs to include; basil, chervil, chives, dill, mint, and parsley

1 small French stick, sliced

¼ cup olive oil

1 tablespoon Chile Oil (see page 119)

salt and pepper

**To Serve:**

extra-virgin olive oil

lemon juice

Serves: 10

**Preparation time:** 12 minutes, plus infusing time

**Cooking time:** 3–4 minutes

# ricotta *crostini*

- In a bowl beat together all the ingredients except for the bread, olive oil, and chile oil. Season to taste with salt and pepper and set aside for at least 1 hour for the flavors to develop.
- Prepare the crostini. Cut the French bread into 20 slices, about ¼ inch thick. Combine the oils and heat together in a large skillet. Fry the bread slices in batches over a gentle heat until lightly golden on both sides. Drain on paper towels and leave to cool.
- Spread a little of the ricotta mixture onto each crostini, drizzle over a little lemon juice and extra-virgin olive oil, and serve at once.

# *pear, endive, and gorgonzola* bruschetta

2 heads Belgian endive

¼ cup butter

2 large ripe pears, cored and sliced

4 slices rustic Italian bread, preferably 1 day old

1 garlic clove, peeled but left whole

2 tablespoons walnut oil

6 oz Gorgonzola cheese, diced

salt and pepper

- Trim the outer leaves from the endive and discard. Cut each one lengthwise into 4 slices.
- Melt half the butter in a skillet and fry the pear slices for 2–3 minutes, until lightly browned on both sides. Remove with a slotted spoon and set aside.
- Add the reserved butter to the skillet and fry the endive for 5 minutes on each side, until softened and golden.
- Meanwhile, toast the bread under a preheated broiler for 1 minute on each side. Rub all over each side with the garlic, then drizzle liberally with the walnut oil.
- Top each bruschetta with the cooked endive and pear slices, place the diced cheese over the pears, and return to the broiler for 1–2 minutes, until bubbling and golden. Serve at once.

Serves: 4

**Preparation time:** 25 minutes

**Cooking time:** 10 minutes

½ x 17¼-oz package frozen puff pastry,
 thawed
1 small Reblochon cheese
1 recipe Egg Glaze (see page 73)
Sweet and Sour Onion Salsa, (see page 92)
 or a sweet chutney, to serve

Serves: 6–8
**Preparation time:** 10 minutes, plus chilling time
**Cooking time:** 20 minutes

# baked Reblochon

*Reblechon is a French semi-soft cow's-milk cheese that is disk shaped, about 5 inches in diameter and roughly 1 inch high.*

- Divide the pastry in half and roll each half out on a lightly floured surface to form a thin square.
- Using a very sharp knife, cut the rind off the cheese. Sit the Reblochon in the middle of 1 pastry square, brush around the cheese with a little egg glaze, and then top with the second pastry square. Press all around the edges to seal well and then trim the pastry to give a 1-inch border.
- Transfer the pastry to a baking sheet and chill for 30 minutes. Preheat the oven to 425°F. Brush the top and sides with the egg glaze and score a criss-cross pattern in the top with a sharp knife. Cut 2 small slits in the top to allow steam to escape.
- Bake for 20 minutes, until the pastry is puffed up and golden. Allow to stand for about 10 minutes, then cut into wedges and serve with salsa or chutney.

1 small head radicchio

4 oz Fontina cheese, rind removed

2–3 tablespoons olive oil

4 slices rustic Italian bread, preferably a day old

1 garlic clove, peeled but left whole

¼ cup Anchoïade (see page 124)

salt and pepper

shavings of fresh Parmesan cheese, to serve

Serves: 4
**Preparation time:** 10 minutes
**Cooking time:** 5 minutes

# broiled radicchio and fontina bruschetta
*with anchoïade*

- Trim the radicchio, discarding any discolored leaves. Cut lengthwise into quarters, wash, and leave to dry. Cut the Fontina into thin slices and slip in between the leaves of the radicchio.
- Heat half the oil in a large skillet, add the radicchio, and fry gently for 2–3 minutes. Carefully turn and cook for a further 2 minutes, until the radicchio is golden and the cheese is melted.
- Meanwhile, toast the bread on both sides and rub all over with the garlic clove, drizzle with a little extra oil, and spread each piece with the Anchoïade. Season with salt and pepper.
- Top each bruschetta with the radicchio, scatter over the Parmesan, and then serve at once.

2 red bell peppers

1 short French bread

1–2 garlic cloves, left whole

½ cup extra-virgin olive oil

1 tablespoon balsamic or
  sherry vinegar

4 ripe tomatoes, sliced

5 oz buffalo mozzarella, sliced

12 large basil leaves

salt and pepper

Serves: 10
**Preparation time:** 30 minutes, plus overnight chilling time
**Cooking time:** 15–20 minutes

# pan bagnat slices

*Pan bagnat, a Niçoise stuffed bread, translates literally as "wet bread." A loaf is hollowed out, soaked with oil, stuffed, and then put back together. It makes a great picnic dish as well as a snack.*

- Preheat the broiler. Place the red peppers on a foil-lined broiler pan and broil for 15–20 minutes, turning frequently, until charred on all sides. Transfer to a plastic bag and leave until cool enough to handle.
- Meanwhile, cut the French bread in half horizontally and scoop out and discard most of the middle, leaving a good ½-inch thick edge. Leave to one side to dry out slightly.
- Peel and seed the peppers over a bowl to catch the juices, and cut the flesh into quarters. Rub the insides of the bread with garlic and drizzle generously with the oil and vinegar.
- Arrange the peppers, tomato slices, mozzarella slices, and basil in layers in one half of the bread, seasoning with salt and pepper. Pour over the reserved pepper juices and any remaining olive oil.
- Replace the remaining half of the bread, wrap tightly in plastic wrap, and chill overnight. Return to room temperature and cut the bread into 1-inch-thick slices to serve.

Serves: 6
**Preparation time:** 20 minutes, plus chilling time
**Cooking time:** 25 minutes

# mini pissaladière

¼ cup olive oil

2 lb onions, thinly sliced

2 garlic cloves, crushed

2 teaspoons chopped fresh
thyme

1 teaspoon salt

1 teaspoon sugar

3 anchovy fillets, halved
lengthwise

6 stoned black olives

3 tablespoons freshly grated
Parmesan cheese

**Pastry:**

1 cup all-purpose flour

¼ teaspoon salt

¼ cup butter, diced

*This classic Provençal tart can be made with a pizza dough as the base or with a pastry case. The topping, however, is always the same: caramelized onions, anchovies, and black olives.*

○ To make the pastry, sift the flour and salt into a bowl and rub in the butter until the mixture resemble fine bread crumbs. Work in 1–2 tablespoons iced water, enough to form a soft dough. Knead lightly and chill for 30 minutes.

○ Heat the oil in a heavy-based skillet and fry the onions, garlic, thyme, salt, and sugar for about 25 minutes, until golden and caramelized. Set aside to cool.

○ Divide the pastry into 6 pieces. Roll each piece out on a lightly floured surface and use to line 6 x 3-inch tartlet pans. Prick the bases with a fork and chill for a further 20 minutes. Preheat the oven to 400°F.

○ Line each pastry case with baking parchment and baking beans, and bake for 15 minutes. Remove the beans and parchment. Leave the oven on.

○ Divide the onion mixture between the pastry cases, and garnish the tops of each one with a cross of anchovies and an olive. Sprinkle over the Parmesan and bake for 10 minutes. Cool on a wire rack and serve warm.

Serves: 4
**Preparation time:** 5 minutes
**Cooking time:** 2 minutes

# anchovy toast
## *with fried green tomatoes*

4 green tomatoes
2–3 tablespoons coarse
    cornflour
2 tablespoon olive oil
4 slices rustic bread

**Anchovy Butter:**
¼ cup butter, softened
½ x 2-oz can anchovies,
    drained and chopped
2 garlic cloves, crushed
1 teaspoon lemon juice
pepper

*Green tomatoes are just unripe red ones, and cooking them is the only way to make use of them. They are often made into a chutney. Here they are coated in cornflour and fried until just soft.*

○ First make the anchovy butter. In a blender or food processor purée the butter, anchovies, garlic, and lemon juice, and season with a little black pepper.

○ Cut the tomatoes into ¼-inch thick slices and coat them with the cornflour. Heat the oil in a non-stick skillet and fry the tomatoes for a few seconds on each side, until golden but not falling apart.

○ Meanwhile, toast the bread on each side either over charcoal or in a broiler or toaster. Spread each slice with the anchovy butter. Top with the cooked tomatoes and serve at once.

Serves: 8
**Preparation time:** 10 minutes
**Cooking time:** 10–15 minutes

# smoked mozzarella and tomato puff tartlets

½ x 17¼-oz package frozen
  puff pastry, thawed
2 large ripe tomatoes
4 oz smoked mozzarella
2 tablespoons Pesto Sauce
  (see page 120)
salt and pepper

*Smoked mozzarella is available from good cheese shops or Italian delicatessens. Use another smoked cheese or plain mozzarella as an alternative.*

- Divide the pastry into 8 equal pieces. Roll each one out thinly on a lightly floured surface and, using a 4-inch pastry cutter, stamp out 8 circles of pastry. Prick the pastry circles with a fork. Place on baking sheets. Preheat the oven to 425°F.
- Cut each tomato into 4 slices and the mozzarella into 8 slices. Spread each circle of pastry with pesto, leaving a thin border around the edges. Top with a slice of tomato and then a slice of mozzarella. Season with salt and pepper.
- Bake the tartlets at the top of the oven for 10–15 minutes, until puffed up and golden. Serve warm.

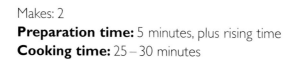

Makes: 2
**Preparation time:** 5 minutes, plus rising time
**Cooking time:** 25 – 30 minutes

# olive foccacia
## *with infused herb oil*

4 cups strong all-purpose flour

2 teaspoons fast acting dry yeast

2 teaspoons sea salt, plus extra for scattering

½ teaspoon superfine sugar

¼ cup Infused Herb Oil (see page 119)

⅓ cup stoned black olives, roughly chopped

extra-virgin olive oil, to serve

○ Sift the flour into the bowl of a food mixer and stir in the yeast, salt, and sugar. Then, with the dough hook turning, gradually add 1⅓ cups warm water and half the infused oil to form a soft dough. Knead for 10 minutes. If you want to make the dough by hand, sift the flour into a bowl and stir in the yeast, salt, and sugar. Make a well in the center and gradually work in half of the infused oil and 1⅓ cups warm water, to form a soft dough. Turn out and knead on a lightly floured surface for 10 minutes.

○ Cover the bowl with plastic wrap and leave to rise in a warm place for about 1 hour, until doubled in size.

○ Punch down the dough, divide in half, and roll each half out to a ½-inch-thick oval. Transfer to 2 greased baking sheets, cover with oiled plastic wrap, and leave to rise for a further 30 minutes. Preheat the oven to 425°F.

○ Remove the plastic wrap and press indentations all over the surface of each dough oval with your fingers. Scatter over a little extra sea salt and the olives, and drizzle over the remaining herb oil.

○ Bake for 25–30 minutes, until risen and golden. Cool slightly and serve warm cut into fingers, with a bowl of extra-virgin olive oil to dip.

Serves: 12
**Preparation time:** 20 minutes, plus marinating and overnight chilling time
**Cooking time:** 20 minutes

# picnic chicken *loaf*

4 boneless, skinless chicken
breasts
4 boneless, skinless chicken
thighs
1 tablespoon lemon juice
½ teaspoon ground turmeric
2 tablespoons olive oil
3 tablespoons chopped fresh
herbs
½ cup pistachio nuts, toasted
and roughly chopped
1 large round eastern-style
sesame loaf, unsliced
1 recipe Chicken Liver Pâté
(see page 92)
salt and pepper

*This stuffed bread is weighed down overnight, which enables it to be cut into wedges to serve. You will need a round loaf approximately 12 inches in diameter.*

- Wash and dry the chicken pieces and rub all over with lemon juice, turmeric, and half the oil, and season with salt and pepper. Leave to marinate for 1 hour.
- Heat the remaining oil in a skillet and fry the chicken for 5 minutes until golden on both sides. Add 5 tablespoons water, bring to a boil, cover, and simmer gently for 15 minutes. Leave to cool in the skillet.
- Remove the chicken and cut it into strips, reserving the pan juices. Place the chicken in a bowl and stir in the herbs, nuts, and reserved juices.
- Cut the top from the loaf and scoop out the middle, leaving a 1-inch-thick shell. (You could make bread crumbs from the filling and freeze for later use if you like.)
- Spoon half the chicken into the hollow bread and carefully spread the pâté over the top. Add the remaining chicken and replace the bread lid. Wrap the loaf tightly in plastic wrap, weigh down with a heavy object, and leave to chill overnight. Cut into wedges to serve.

Serves: 4
**Preparation time:** 25 minutes
**Cooking time:** 5 minutes

# *eggplant and* pepper layer

1 eggplant
¼ cup extra-virgin olive oil
2 large red bell peppers,
   quartered
4 slices day-old rustic bread
1 garlic clove, peeled but left
   whole
1 ripe tomato, halved
6 oz goat cheese
pepper

- Preheat the broiler. Cut the eggplant into ¼-inch slices, brush with oil, and broil for 2–3 minutes on each side, until charred and tender. Let cool.
- Broil the peppers for 4–5 minutes each side. Transfer to a plastic bag and let soften for 15 minutes. Peel and discard the charred skins, and cut the flesh into wide strips.
- Toast the bread on both sides and rub all over the surface first with the garlic clove and then with the tomato.
- Brush over any remaining oil and layer the eggplant and peppers over the toast. Cut the goat cheese into 8 slices and arrange 2 slices on top of each toast. Season with pepper.
- Return to the broiler for 1–2 minutes, until the cheese is bubbling and melted, and serve immediately.

# *spinach and ricotta* tartlets

1½ cups all-purpose flour
a pinch of salt
6 tablespoons butter, diced
¼ cup freshly grated Parmesan
   cheese
3–4 tablespoons cold water

**Filling:**
4 oz frozen leaf spinach,
   thawed and squeezed dry
7 oz ricotta cheese
2 tablespoons freshly grated
   Parmesan cheese
a little grated nutmeg
2 eggs, beaten
¼ cup light cream
salt and pepper

- Sift the flour and salt into a bowl and, using your fingertips, rub in the butter until the mixture resembles fine bread crumbs. Stir in the Parmesan and then gradually work in enough water to form a soft dough. Knead lightly, wrap in plastic wrap, and leave to rest for 30 minutes.
- Divide the rested dough into 6 and roll each piece out to line a 3½-inch tartlet pan. Prick the base with a fork and chill for 20 minutes.
- Meanwhile, prepare the filling. Place all the ingredients in a bowl and mix until well blended. Season well with salt and pepper. Preheat the oven to 400°F.
- Line the pastry cases with baking parchment and baking beans, and bake for 10 minutes. Remove the foil and beans, and bake for a further 10 minutes, until the pastry is crisp and golden.
- Divide the filling between the cases, return to the oven, and bake for 20 minutes more, until risen and firm to the touch. Cool slightly and serve warm.

Serves: 6
**Preparation time:** 30 minutes, plus resting and chilling time
**Cooking time:** 40 minutes

Makes: 6
**Preparation time:** 15 minutes
**Cooking time:** 6 minutes

1 baguette or ciabatta loaf
3–4 tablespoons extra-virgin olive oil
⅔ cup pesto (see page 120)

**Topping:**
⅓ cup stoned black olives
2 tomatoes, peeled
½ small onion
1 garlic clove, peeled
½ tablespoon chopped fresh parsley
½ tablespoon chopped fresh basil
10–12 anchovy fillets
salt and pepper
6 basil leaves, to garnish

# crostini *with mediterranean topping*

- Make the topping. Combine the olives, tomatoes, onion, garlic, and herbs. Preheat the oven to 400°F. Cut the bread at an angle into 6 x ½-inch slices, arrange on an oiled baking sheet, and bake for 5–6 minutes, until the bread is golden brown.
- Spread a layer of pesto on each slice, then spoon the topping mixture evenly onto the bread. Arrange 2–3 anchovy fillets on each slice. Garnish with basil leaves and serve immediately.

# prosciutto and mozzarella toast

4 thick slices farmhouse bread
1 tablespoon olive oil
4 slices prosciutto
2 ripe plum tomatoes, sliced
8 oz mozzarella cheese, sliced
1 teaspoon dried oregano
¼ cup stoned black olives, halved
salt and pepper

- Lightly toast the bread on both sides and transfer to a baking sheet.
- Heat the olive oil in a skillet, add the prosciutto, and fry over a high heat for 1–2 minutes, until crisp and golden.
- Preheat the oven to 450°F. Arrange the prosciutto over the toast and top with slices of tomato and mozzarella. Scatter over the oregano and top with the olives. Season with a little salt and pepper and then bake for 10 minutes. Serve hot.

Serves: 4
**Preparation time:** 10 minutes
**Cooking time:** 10 minutes

Although several of the recipes within this chapter are accompaniments for, or integral to, other recipes in the book, the Bagna Cauda can make a splendid centerpiece for a dinner party appetizer, and the Smoky Tomato Salsa is a great spread for toasted ciabatta or a French bread.

# sauces, oils, and dips

Makes: approximately 1⅓ cups
**Preparation time:** 10 minutes
**Cooking time:** 5 minutes, plus infusing time

# *smoky* **tomato salsa**

4 ripe tomatoes
1 small onion, finely chopped
1 red chile, deseeded and
 finely chopped
1 garlic clove, crushed
¼ cup chopped fresh cilantro
2 tablespoons extra-virgin
 olive oil
1 tablespoon lime juice
salt and pepper

*The charring of the tomato skins adds a wonderfully intense smoky flavor to this salsa.*

○ Using tongs, hold the tomatoes over a gas flame and char well on all sides. Cool slightly, and then peel and discard the skin. Halve the tomatoes, remove the seeds, and finely chop the flesh.

○ Put the tomato flesh into a bowl and stir in all the remaining ingredients. Season to taste, cover, and leave to infuse for several hours. Serve as an accompaniment or with vegetable crudités or tortilla chips.

# *three flavored* **oils**

*Pour a little amount of any of the following oils into a small dish and serve with chunks of bread as a pre-dinner snack.*

## chile oil

4 dried red chiles

2 garlic cloves

1⅓ cups extra-virgin olive oil

○ Place the chiles and garlic in a clean bottle and add the oil. Seal the bottle and store in a cool dark place for 1 week. Use as required. The oil will keep for up to 3 months.

Makes: 1⅓ cups
**Preparation time:** 2 minutes

## herb oil

1 sprig rosemary, bruised

1 sprig thyme, bruised

2 bay leaves, bruised

6 black peppercorns, bruised

1⅓ cups extra-virgin olive oil

○ Feed the herbs and peppercorns into a clean bottle, pour in the olive oil, and seal the bottle. Leave in a cool dark place (but not the refrigerator) for 1 week for the flavors to develop. Use as required. The oil will keep for up to 1 week.

Makes: 1⅓ cups
**Preparation time:** 2 minutes

## infused herb oil

2 sprigs fresh rosemary

2 sprigs fresh thyme

2 fresh red chiles

2 garlic cloves

2 strips lemon rind

¼ teaspoon fennel seeds, lightly bruised

6 black peppercorns, bruised

1⅓ cups extra-virgin olive oil

○ Place all the ingredients in a small, heavy-based saucepan and warm over a very low heat for 20 minutes. Do not allow the oil to boil.

○ Leave the oil to cool completely and then transfer to a clean jar or bottle. Seal and store in the refrigerator. Use as required. The oil will keep for up to 1 week.

Makes: 1⅓ cups
**Preparation time:** 5 minutes
**Cooking time:** 20 minutes

Makes: approximately 1⅓ cups
**Preparation time:** 5 minutes

# salsa verde

2 garlic cloves
1 cup flat leaf parsley (leaves only)
½ cup each basil leaves, dill, mint, chives, and chervil
1 tablespoon rinsed capers
1 tablespoon red wine vinegar
1 teaspoon Dijon mustard
1⅓ cups extra-virgin olive oil
salt and pepper

○ Put the garlic, herbs, and capers in a blender or food processor and pulse briefly until the herbs are finely chopped. Add the vinegar and mustard.

○ With the motor running, blend in the oil through the feeder funnel to form a vibrant green sauce. Season to taste with salt and pepper and store in a sealed jar in the refrigerator. Use within 1 week.

# pesto

1 garlic clove, chopped
½ teaspoon sea salt
1 cup basil leaves
1 cup pine nuts
½ cup extra-virgin olive oil
2 tablespoons freshly grated Parmesan cheese
pepper

○ Put all the ingredients except the cheese in a blender or food processor and pulse briefly until smooth. Transfer to a bowl and stir in the Parmesan. Season to taste with pepper.

Makes: approximately ⅔ cup
**Preparation time:** 5 minutes

Makes: approximately ⅔ cup
**Preparation time:** 5 minutes

¾ cup stoned black olives

2 garlic cloves, sliced

4 anchovy fillets in oil, drained
and chopped

2 tablespoons chopped fresh
parsley

1 tablespoon chopped fresh
thyme

6 – 8 tablespoons olive oil

pepper

# tapenade

- Place all the ingredients except the oil and pepper in a blender or food processor and pulse until you have a fairly smooth paste.
- Transfer to a bowl and stir in the oil. Season with pepper to taste and store in a screw-top jar in the refrigerator for up to 1 week.

# skordalia

*This is a Greek garlic sauce and is served as a dip to accompany cooked meats, fish, and vegetables.*

- Cook the potatoes in lightly salted, boiling water for 8–10 minutes until done.
- Drain well, return to the pot and heat gently to dry out the potatoes. Leave to cool.
- Using a vegetable mouli or potato ricer, finely mash the potatoes until smooth, then stir in the garlic, lemon juice, and salt.
- Very gradually whisk in the olive oil to form a thick fluffy mayonnaise sauce, and season to taste with pepper.

8 oz potatoes, cubed

3 garlic cloves, crushed

1 tablespoon lemon juice

½ teaspoon sea salt

⅔ cup extra-virgin olive oil

pepper

Makes: approximately 1¼ cups
**Preparation time:** 5 minutes
**Cooking time:** 10 minutes

2 tablespooons unsalted butter

2 garlic cloves, crushed

½ x 2-oz can anchovies in oil, drained and
   roughly chopped

½ cup olive oil

pepper

a large selection fresh baby vegetables,
   trimmed and blanched as necessary, to serve

Serves: 4
**Preparation time:** 10 minutes
**Cooking time:** 10–15 minutes

# bagna cauda

*This is a hot garlic and anchovy sauce from the Piedmont region of Italy. It is served at the table in its cooking pot surrounded by platters of raw and cooked vegetables.*

- Put the butter and garlic into a small saucepan and heat gently to melt the butter. Cook over a low heat for 2 minutes or until the garlic is softened but not browned (or it will become bitter).
- Add the anchovies, stir once, and then whisk in the oil. Season with salt and pepper. Continue to cook over a low heat for 10 minutes, stirring from time to time. Transfer the sauce to a warmed bowl and serve immediately with the selection of vegetables.

Makes: approximately ⅔ cup
**Preparation time:** 5 minutes, plus soaking time

2 × 2-oz cans anchovies in oil,
   drained
⅔ cup milk
2 tablespoons pine nuts,
   toasted
2 garlic cloves, crushed
2 tablespoons chopped fresh
   basil
1 tablespoon lemon juice
¼ teaspoon cayenne pepper
2 tablespoons olive oil
pepper

# anchoïade

- Place the anchovy fillets in a bowl, pour over the milk, and set aside to soak for 10 minutes. Drain and pat dry.
- Roughly chop the anchovies, place in a blender or food processor with all the remaining ingredients except the oil, and pulse until smooth.
- Transfer the paste to a bowl, stir in the oil, and season to taste with pepper. Store the Anchoïade in a screw-top jar in the refrigerator for up to 1 week.

2 × 2-oz cans anchovies in oil,
   drained
⅔ cup pint milk
¼ cup finely chopped canned
   or bottled pimento
½ cup fresh bread crumbs
2 garlic cloves, crushed
2 tablespoons chopped fresh
   parsley
1 tablespoon red wine vinegar
¼ teaspoon cayenne pepper
2 tablespoons olive oil
pepper

*variation*
# anchovy and pimento spread

- Use the same method as above, adding the pimentos, bread crumbs, and red wine vinegar to the blender.

Makes: approximately ¾ cup
**Preparation time:** 8–10 minutes, plus soaking time

Makes: approximately 1¾ cups
**Preparation time:** 2 minutes

# mayonnaise

2 egg yolks
1 teaspoon lemon juice
1 teaspoon Dijon mustard
pinch of sugar
½ teaspoon sea salt
1¾ cups olive oil
pepper

○ Put the egg yolks, lemon juice, mustard, sugar, and salt into a blender or food processor, season with pepper, and pulse briefly until pale and creamy.

○ With the blade running, gradually pour in the oil through the funnel until the mixture is thick, glossy, and pale. You may need to add a little boiling water to the mixture if it becomes too thick.

○ Transfer to a bowl, taste and adjust the seasoning, if necessary. Cover with cling film and refrigerate until required. This will keep for up to 3 days.

*variation*
# aïoli

2 egg yolks
2–4 garlic cloves, crushed
½ teaspoon sea salt
1 tablespoon white wine
  vinegar
300 ml/½ pint olive oil
pepper

○ Combine all the ingredients except the oil in a blender or food processor, season with pepper, and continue as above.

Makes: approximately 1¾ cups
**Preparation time:** 3 minutes

# index